The Creative Arts in Dementia Care

by the same author

Soul and Spirit in Dance Movement Psychotherapy
A Transpersonal Approach
Jill Hayes
Foreword by Daria Halprin
ISBN 978 1 84905 308 2
eISBN 978 0 85700 649 3

of related interest

Creativity and Communication in Persons with Dementia
A Practical Guide
John Killick and Claire Craig
ISBN 978 1 84905 113 2
eISBN 978 0 85700 301 0

Connecting through Music with People with Dementia
A Guide for Caregivers
Robin Rio
ISBN 978 1 84310 905 1
eISBN 978 1 84642 725 1

Remembering Yesterday, Caring Today
Reminiscence in Dementia Care: A Guide to Good Practice
Pam Schweitzer and Errollyn Bruce
ISBN 978 1 84310 649 4
eISBN 978 1 84642 804 3

The Creative Arts in Palliative Care
Edited by Nigel Hartley and Malcolm Payne
ISBN 978 1 84310 591 6
eISBN 978 1 84642 802 9

Healing Arts Therapies and Person-Centred Dementia Care
Edited by Anthea Innes and Karen Hatfield
ISBN 978 1 84310 038 6
eISBN 978 1 84642 302 4

Puppetry in Dementia Care
Connecting through Creativity and Joy
Karrie Marshall
ISBN 978 1 84905 392 1
eISBN 978 0 85700 848 0

The Creative Arts in Dementia Care
Practical Person-Centred Approaches and Ideas

Jill Hayes with Sarah Povey
Foreword by Shaun McNiff

Jessica Kingsley *Publishers*
London and Philadelphia

First published in 2011
by Jessica Kingsley Publishers
73 Collier Street
London N1 9BE, UK
and
400 Market Street, Suite 400
Philadelphia, PA 19106, USA

www.jkp.com

Library of Congress Cataloging in Publication Data
Hayes, Jill, Dr.
  The creative arts in dementia care : practical person-centred approaches and ideas / Jill
Hayes with Sarah Povey ; foreword by Shaun McNiff.
    p. cm.
  Includes bibliographical references and index.
  ISBN 978-1-84905-056-2 (alk. paper)
  1. Dementia--Patients--Care. 2. Arts--Therapeutic use. 3. Dementia--Treatment. I. Povey,
Sarah. II. Title.
  RC521.H395 2010
  616.8'3--dc22
                                    2010011431

British Library Cataloguing in Publication Data
A CIP catalogue record for this book is available from the British Library

ISBN 978 1 84905 056 2
eISBN 978 0 85700 251 8

Villanelle – with apologies to Dylan Thomas

Do not go raging into that good night
Do not regret you've had your glory day
Come, dance into the glory of the Light.

Wiser than you have raged against their plight
Riding the thermals you have made your way
Do not go raging into that good night.

Many good people set the world alight
Better to set the rules than to obey
Come, dance into the glory of the Light.

Wildly the dance put demons into flight
As faced with joyfulness they could not stay
Do not go raging into that good night.

Pausing to breathe your last upon the height
Rejoice as to the grave you make your way
Come, dance into the glory of the Light.

Mothers, shed tears of joy for life's insight
Blessing the earth wherein your bones will lay
Do not go raging into that good night
Come, dance into the glory of the Light.

Cathy French, March 2009

Cathy's daughter writes:

My Mum was a bright and creative lady who kept herself mentally active right up until the end of her life. This poem was the result of an exercise set out in Stephen Fry's (2005), *The Ode Less Travelled: Unlocking the Poet Within*. Mum's positive attitude towards death helped change many of her friends' and her family's opinions of it, and ultimately made it easier for us all to come to terms with hers.

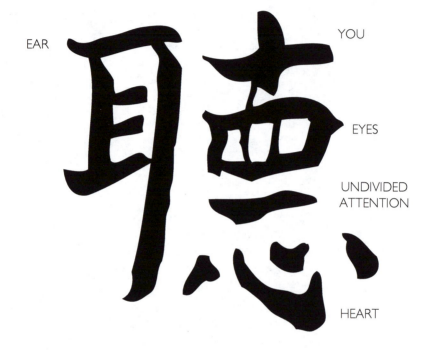

EAR

YOU

EYES

UNDIVIDED
ATTENTION

HEART

This Chinese character (to listen) is central to our work because it implies lack of division between self and others when listening with the heart.

Contents

Acknowledgements

There are many wonderful people who have inspired me to work from my creative heart, too many to name here. But to all of you who have influenced my practice, I want to say thank you for reaching out to me and changing me. In particular, I want to thank my mother, Dyllys Hayes, and my husband, Paul Wilson, for showing me the meaning of enduring love, and my dear friend Melanie Brierley, for being there with creativity, humour and joy on all occasions. I want also to thank Joan Brooks, Marie Price, Andrea Linell and Jan Spafford for creative times spent together, and my friends Marie-Therese Arnoux, Jo Bentley, Katie Curtis, Geoff Ellis, 'Mac', Mhairi McLuskie, Christine Neilson and Jean Park for all the love and laughter. I mustn't forget the infusion of boyish energy in the form of Finny, Lawrie, Owain and Theo Wilson, who brighten my world with humour and rhythm. For work in therapy and the creative arts I thank Mike Boxhall, compassionate teacher and friend in stillness, Rod Paton, intuitive musicmaker, Claudine Peronne, who shakes the dust from my eyes with her writings, her clay figures and her images, Mary Nonde, artmaker and dancer, Anna Halprin for her visions and participations in nature, Anne Colvin and Sarah Povey for the joyful experience of creative arts co-facilitation, and Jill Cutsforth whose devotion to the care of people with dementia included the art of storytelling. I dedicate this book to Kay.

Sarah gives heartfelt thanks to: my husband, Edward Couzens-Lake, for his constant love, patience and encouragement; Ilona Griffiths and Muriel Gilbert for their unwavering belief and faith in me when I first began my work in this field; my husband, mother and two dear friends, Trudi Hatherell and Judi Smith for their editing advice and guidance; my first music teacher, Mrs Gilliver, whose enthusiasm and energy for singing greatly inspires me still; Jill Hayes for her continuing support, understanding and encouragement in my work. I also want to thank the relatives who have given me permission to write about my experience with their loved ones, and to all those I have sung with, and continue to sing with, who have taught me so much. I would like to dedicate my contributions to my mother, Emmie, whose innate compassion for older people is an inspiration.

Foreword

Jill Hayes and Sarah Povey have made an important contribution to helping health professionals see creative expression as a necessity for those afflicted with dementia. They convincingly demonstrate how there is a 'core self' in each person which can be renewed through the arts, enabling people experiencing cognitive and physical impairments to access areas of creative vitality and to continuously recreate themselves when they may no longer be able to interact with others in familiar ways.

This book corresponds completely to the authors' encouragement of 'heartfelt' expression. It models how to truly *be* with other people with impaired cognitive functions; how to let ourselves witness and adjust to their worlds which can give so much to our own.

Dementia is approached as 'a condition of living' which can teach us all how to become more completely immersed in the present moment, to appreciate the joy and humanity offered by the most elemental aspects of life, to dream with what we have and to value what tends to go unseen. As I have discovered with the most severe losses of cognition, we can explore elemental ways to communicate and affirm human dignity and the life force through touch and the perception of bodily reflexes. Dementia has this potential to restore appreciation for basic conditions of life and create opportunities to use faculties that have been dormant and underutilized.

Those of us who have worked with people experiencing dementia or who have loved ones living with this condition understand how adjustments need to be made with regard to expectations, and how we embrace what people are able to do in order to interact with them. Relating to others with dementia may thus require communication in different and more inventive ways, ranging from play without words to simply learning how to sit in silence while concentrating on the present moment. This focus on changes in attitude experienced by caregivers is a primary theme of the book, which underscores the importance of the act of witnessing in a relationship with another person. This might be considered other-centred contemplative practice, in which dementia becomes an opening to an expansion of experience.

Turning the tables on the difficulties presented by dementia does not deny the pain and feelings of loss they inflict. I ask myself how we can create with the shadows of experience and do something with them that affirms life and the love felt for those who are now living in a different place; how we can channel the despair or anger felt about these losses into productive expressions that do bring improvement in feelings. Thus the core of this work with the arts in dementia care is pragmatic and challenging. As Sarah Povey says in describing the losses associated with dementia and the changes they require, 'It is us that needs to make the shift to join *them*, not expect them to return to us.'

I strongly support the book's embrace of all of the arts, which offers many therapeutic advantages when addressing deficits of the mind and body. As one or more aspects of thought and communication become impaired, others can be tapped to compensate and stimulate areas of deficit. The mind operates via an interdependence of the senses, and the range of modalities of communication and perception suggested in this book – from the visual arts, poetry, dance, music, and drama – uniquely furthers both quality of life and therapeutic treatment. The senses support and inform one another in all aspects of human expression and especially when there are difficulties with certain functions.

This approach to multiplicity in the arts is also in sync with the book's affirmation of group expression and how working with others creates a collective effect which enables someone to do things that are not possible in isolation. As the authors suggest, authentic and soulful expression creates an atmosphere, a creative space pervaded by a sense of sanctity as well as a vitality, which acts upon everyone in it. Art's healing powers are often environmental, and Jill Hayes correctly emphasizes the importance of staff participating in health settings along with family members and friends, a cooperative engagement that activates an ecology of creative expression which emits art's healing elements.

I hope that this book inspires the most pervasive infusion of creative vitality into our society. The authors suggest numerous ways for engaging others in imaginative expressions, all of which are grounded in the body's movement. In addition to bringing these art-making activities to others, readers can also practise them, something I recommend as the best way to get started. Experience with the arts and healing constantly affirms the importance of therapists and helpers becoming co-participants in the creative process.

From the inception of my involvement with the arts in healing over 40 years ago, I have been convinced that their potential will only be realized as the result of wider participation in all sectors of society. Although my personal work and the growth of the creative arts therapies has been significantly informed by the practice of psychotherapy, I have always been committed to broader engagement and realizing the role the arts can play in public health for all people. Art heals in many ways, with mental health being part of a whole spectrum of features constituting well being in body, mind, spirit, relationships and community life. I believe that creative exercise for the mind and body is as important to health as physical fitness, and that we must find ways to build professions that support this aim while also making it possible for people everywhere to participate.

However, when inviting universal participation, I see that many people resist involvement in the arts for reasons that include a sense of inferiority, a perceived lack of talent, bad past experiences and a general sense that the arts are only for those with the prerequisite training and skills. In contrast, the authors of this book and I believe in more comprehensive access to creative expression, which can be likened to the necessity of breathing and essential physical movement.

A simple focus tends to generate greater depth of expression. As Jill Hayes says, 'All movements can be considered a dance.' Our goal as leaders of the creative process is actually to help people forget their preoccupations and inhibitions for a while, to lighten their grip on the controls and let things happen as spontaneously as they often do in childhood. As one woman in the early stages of dementia said about her experience described in the book, 'I don't know what happened but the music got inside my body and I just had to dance.'

The authors also emphasize how the arts can get inside communities and organizations when staff members become involved. To increase creative energy in different sectors of society we need to expand our assumptions about health and the values of artistic expression. I urge people to begin by introducing the standard of 'good enough' art and the importance of expressions that convey a person's unique ways of moving – an individual's creative DNA conveying a beauty defined by its distinct qualities that must be distinguished from those of another person. If you can move, I say, you can paint, write, sing, dance and act. Just begin to move, and expression will emerge from what you do and you will have a contagious impact on others.

Everything about artistic expression is incremental and interactive. Movements build upon one another, as contrasted to the notion that an artistic composition is conceived in the mind and then depicted or performed according to a pre-existing idea or script. One gesture influences another in shaping every art form. The same thing happens amongst people participating in the creative process. Immersion in the creative expression of others generates a life-enhancing circulation of creativity, often bringing corresponding benefits to those who serve as both professional helpers and volunteers.

The Creative Arts in Dementia Care makes major contributions to realizing a more complete participation in the creative process. The book's focus on dementia, a condition of ageing that can afflict any human being, offers an inclusive invitation for all people to participate in the arts in a way that will advance art healing as a vital element of public health. I have observed how people from all sectors of life spontaneously turn to the arts in response to life-threatening illness (their own and that of loved ones), loss of life and tragedy, but it is dementia and ageing where we can find the most unifying of human conditions, the great equalizer, perhaps showing the way to a return to the natural expression of childhood often invoked by the authors.

As the number of people ageing in our world increases, the use of the arts with the elderly is becoming a major frontier for the arts and healing. My hope is that rather than just lamenting the loss of creative imagination and spontaneous expression associated with the early years, we will begin to look to the opportunities offered by our lives in the present, integrating expressions of childhood and ageing which may also enrich everything that exists between them.

Shaun McNiff
Lesley University, Cambridge, Massachusetts

Introduction

To begin

If you are disillusioned with the situation of people with dementia in your country, you are not alone. There are many who long to transform the care and treatment for dementia, bringing humanity back to those who are sometimes considered as beyond help and beyond reach. I have written this book in the belief that in some way person-centred creative arts can contribute much to the transformation of dementia care. The person-centred creative approaches and ideas which are given here can be easily applied by anyone ready to give creativity a go.

The ideas and approaches are taken from the professional practice of creative arts therapies in the context of dementia care. I am trained professionally as a dance movement psychotherapist and my colleague Sarah Povey as a voice movement therapist. Over the years we have both collected a number of case studies which we believe illustrate the effectiveness of the creative arts in dementia care. We think that many of the approaches and ideas which inform our practice may be applied by a wide range of professionals interested in developing creative therapeutic care for people with dementia.

How do the creative arts reach people with dementia?

The creative arts can reach even the most cognitively impaired people because they depend upon something other than the intellect. Creativity comes from somewhere beyond the intellect; it flows from an intuitive non-rational place in the body and mind, so we can tap into the creativity of everyone, no matter how much their logic or sequential memory has been disturbed.

The creative arts have the power to stir feeling and memory when a person seems to have lost contact with chronological time. The arts seem to reach below the conscious level of experience and move underground towards a hidden depth memory, accessing the feelings stowed away. In so doing they can reconnect a person to their feeling life and most importantly to the meaning that was made at a particular moment in time. Even when that meaning can no longer be understood or conveyed in words, it can still warm the heart.

It seems important to make a space for people with dementia to have their feelings, whether these are feelings from past times or feelings about their present experience. Some feelings will be pleasurable, some will inevitably be painful. Life seems so full of loss and confusion, fear and frustration in states of dementia and it seems vital that such feelings are acknowledged and listened to. People with dementia can often express their feelings through the arts when words are difficult to find.

Dementia is a heartbreaking condition. The context of memory disintegrates and sabotages our ability to connect in the present moment. Yet still it is the heart's yearning to belong (O'Donohue 1999). Dementia cuts us adrift; we may feel scared, confused and lost, drifting away from the safety of the shore of identity.

The creative arts can remind us who we were, which can bring comfort. The arts bring the memories alive again and rejoin us with the feelings of security and involvement which we may have had as an independent adult. Often creative arts work focuses upon reminiscence, helping people to reconnect with their past life and to feel some sense of continuity.

Yet equally important is the way the creative arts can help us to feel peace and connection in the here and now. They can help us to relax and be quietly present with our sensations and emotional feelings now. Some say they reconnect us with that pulse of life which lies underneath all else, and this in itself is healing (Boxhall 1999).

Sarah and I believe that the creative arts can serve this dual function. They can help to link us back both to the shore of identity and to the core of our being. They keep us in contact with our hearts. They can help to keep us afloat and connected (to self and others) while we change from who we once were to who we are now.

As we change we are often moved from the home we lived in to a new home which is unfamiliar and strange. It is important that as we leave our external home we keep relationship with our inner home which is the home of our hearts. When our rational faculties are failing, the inner core (coeur/heart) still lives on, needing attention and nourishment. We argue here that the creative arts can have a substantial part to play in attending to the needs of the heart. They can provide a space for the emotional life of a person to be felt and to be expressed. In singing and listening to song, in dancing or watching others dance, in painting or watching others paint, people with dementia are given the chance to connect with their feeling life, their sensations and their emotions.

The evidence

We use living examples of practice taken from real case studies to illustrate how the creative arts can work in person-centred dementia care. These case study examples reflect upon the process and the efficacy of the creative arts with people with dementia. They reflect upon the value of the creative arts in achieving communication with people with dementia and in promoting their wellbeing. They aim to show how the creative arts can be used effectively. They record the responses of the people with dementia as evidence of efficacy. All names used are pseudonyms to protect anonymity.

In these case studies, people with dementia have been witnessed and listened to during their participation in creative arts processes. Responses have been recorded carefully and sensitively. We witnessed bodily responses, emotional responses, imaginative responses, interactive responses. We also noticed our own responses, which helped us to discover and therefore free ourselves from our own (sometimes prejudiced) attitudes towards the person concerned. The close, intuitive and self-reflective (reflexive) nature of witnessing in this creative arts work is a valuable adjunct to the keen empathic observations made in Dementia Care Mapping (DCM), originated and developed by the Bradford Dementia Group at Bradford University. DCM is an action research intervention incorporating the perspective of the person with dementia in the improvement of care.[1]

Creative listening with body and heart

The concept of witnessing in the creative arts is very valuable in dementia care. It takes the observation beyond what is physically perceived

---

1   To find out more about the group you can visit it's website at www.brad.ac.uk/health/
     dementia.

(behavioural observation) and empathically felt. It cultivates the important skill of self-awareness, which is essential to person-centred practice. The person who witnesses someone with dementia during creative arts processes has the chance to become aware of the judgements they make about the other. We tend to overlay the creative responses of the other with associations and meanings which most certainly arrive from our own life experience. In becoming aware of these judgements, we can see how they limit the creativity of the other. We have the chance to let go of the judgements, and welcome the creative response of the other as an expression which we can appreciate but perhaps never quite fully understand. By noticing the reductive judgements we make in interaction with people with dementia, we can come closer to their original stories, to their present truth.

Witnessing not only frees the witnessed from the confinement of our judgements, it also frees us as witnesses from these limits of mind. We can move closer with congruence and transparency to the person with dementia, and we can enjoy the depth connection which this facilitates. This person-centred meditative process is frequently present in the creative arts activities suggested here. It is a way of getting past the block to relationship created by dementia; a way of being with the core of the person with dementia, still there despite the mental confusion and chaos.

Witnessing helps to increase self-awareness and removes the barriers which separate us from the other. Letting go of judgements, we can be present with another in the place of the heart (Pearmain 2001). We can see them more clearly and receive their communication more readily. This quality of heartfelt openness to the other is frequently missing in care work and yet it is most vital to care. We must never forget that we are caring for the whole human being, not just the physical body. All human beings feel their aloneness in their hearts and need others to meet them with their own hearts, to identify with them, to be emotionally and honestly available to them. One of the worst things about being in care must surely be the sense of being alone, that no one understands or even wants to. Imagine how much worse this must be for the person with dementia with all the confusion that this disease creates. So we must invest more in care of the soul (Moore 1992), if we are to develop our practice.

The concept of witnessing used here in the creative arts is influenced by the practice of authentic movement, from the field of dance movement psychotherapy (Musicant 1994, 2001). Developing a 'felt-sense': an awareness of the body, was also actively promoted by Eugene Gendlin (1981) in person-centred practice. Here we recommend 'listening to' our body, to notice how we are feeling inside as we carry out our work with people with dementia. We may uncover a range of feelings, some sad, some happy. Some of these feelings may be ours on the day, feelings that we bring with us to work as a result of life outside, whereas some feelings may arise from our contact with the person with dementia, because the feelings in them resonate with us and we feel them as our own. These feelings may be first perceived kinesthetically and later emotionally, or they may become clear through art-making. Awareness of emotions can help to release them. Letting them go, we can find deeper levels of contact and relationship.

Sensitivity to the body can bring about a depth connection with self and others, a connection which moves deeper than identity and does not therefore depend upon an intact chronological sense of time. Sensitivity to the body and to the heart brings about a felt connection with the person with dementia, which does not rely upon the orientation of words.

Activities

The case study scenarios presented in the book are full of activities for you to try out. They are also rich in contextual and relational processes which can emerge through immersion in the activities. The word activity implies action, movement, spending time in productive making. In a way, it is the wrong word for the ideas and approaches outlined here, because they offer more than the term contains. They show how to facilitate a creative process as well as giving suggestions for things to do, and rather than active busyness, we often recommend inactivity or 'stillness', listening and witnessing quietly in the midst of a creative process.

The Skills for Care project

Skills for Care provides funding to support the training standards and development needs of social care staff in England. We have recently both been involved in a Skills for Care dementia project seeking to enhance dementia care by inducting care staff and managers in the use of the creative arts. This training brought home to us the essential part which creativity has to play in the continuing professional development and supervision of care staff and managers. We began to see how important it was for staff to have the opportunity to develop their own creativity in order to encourage creativity in others.

At the beginning of the project so many staff would say 'I'm not creative,' 'I can't draw,' 'I can't dance' and 'I can't sing.' But by the end they had changed their minds and would say things like 'Well I may not be a professional artist, but I *can* express my feelings in pictures, a song and a dance.' This is in fact the point of the arts in therapeutic care. The arts are simply ways of expressing feelings and of connecting to each another.

The staff participating in this project gained confidence in their own creativity. Creativity is different to aesthetic ability. We are all born creative; it is innate, it is in our blood. If we can tell the intellect to stand aside and trust our intuition we will find our creativity ready to lead. If we are connected to our body, our feelings and to each other, we know what to do intuitively. We step into the playful shoes of the child, moving with ease, with lightness, for the sake of having fun.

Having a playful attitude seems to bring with it creative authority. When we play we do not question the validity of what we do or make. Playing seems to free us of the judgements which steal our thunder. The staff involved in the project frequently commented that they had enjoyed themselves, they had felt free and expressive and that this was a quality which would impact positively and creatively upon their work.

In addition, the creative arts training group often became a therapeutic container for the staff to express feelings which sapped their creativity and prevented them from being actively aware of the feelings of others. Feelings could be expressed through movement, image and voice in a safe way. Therapeutic safety can be enhanced by the arts which have the capacity to contain painful feelings, often hard for us to contemplate or express through words alone (Levine 2009). In feedback, staff expressed an understanding that by becoming more emotionally aware, they could be more self-aware and actively engaged with people with dementia.

The book has certainly been influenced by the success of the Skills for Care dementia project. As a result of the project, participants are integrating person-centred creative ideas and approaches into their work. Some are dancing, some are learning new songs, some are simply being more spontaneously creative in everyday interactions.

A significant and unexpected outcome of the project was that participants felt the training enhanced relationships between staff members. The reality of dementia care in the United Kingdom is that many care workers are from other countries and there is a need for mutual respect for diversity among staff members in order to work together successfully. The mutual listening promoted by dance movement, art and song enabled people with cultural differences to learn about each other's feelings and perceptions. From a place of shared understanding through the arts they felt more in tune with one another, more like a team.

Often there is irritation when a person from a different culture behaves differently to us. There seems to be a desire for the other to behave in the same way as us. However, reality is different; the reality is difference. Some cultures emphasize self-expression for both males and females, some cultures do not. Some cultures promote tactile relationships, some do not. While we are speaking out in this book for creative approaches and ideas involving awareness, expression and depth relationship, we also realize that some of these ideas may sometimes clash with cultural expectations. The way forward, as always. is through listening and sensitivity as well as clarity of purpose. If for some care staff it is difficult to sing or dance with others, we can find out how they can more comfortably make contact with the feeling life of the person with dementia and make a more meaningful relationship with them. I have witnessed how someone who found it difficult to sing and dance expressively was completely at ease while sitting with another gently and with full body presence gently massaging their hands.

Of course it is not just the culture we are from which impacts upon the way we behave and what we feel comfortable with. We all possess unique ways of being in the world which are present regardless of culture. It is important to acknowledge and accept our own ways of being so that we can be congruent with others. While we may challenge ourselves sometimes to change, we must not force ourselves into ways of being which cause us to flee emotionally and therefore create pretence; this makes the exchange superficial and dissatisfying, and destroys the intention to increase contact.

We believe that the wellbeing of staff is important in dementia care and that wellbeing is promoted when we listen to the inner life of the person. As in any organization, the wellbeing of staff contributes to the quality of the service imparted to the service users; that in being listened to, we cultivate the ability to listen to ourselves and others. Participants in the Skills for Care creative arts activities felt better in themselves and felt more intuitively open to others.

Emotional availability through creativity

We are proposing that emotional and creative sensitivity is essential in dementia care. We acknowledge the necessity of practical nursing care but emphasize alongside this another necessity: to attend to the person's inner life. We feel that it is important to care for the soul as well as the body of the person with dementia. In order to do this we need to develop a relationship with our own emotional life. It is through this emotional awareness that we become able to be responsive to the emotional life of another.

We have found that we become more aware of our emotions through creative practice. Images seem to carry with them the feelings which we cannot let ourselves feel. This is why artistic creativity has become an established method of encountering and coming to terms with our feelings (McNiff 2004). Carl Jung (1979, 1990) believed that creativity is a basic healing drive in human nature. He described it as an instinct. Here we call it a life force: an organic healing impulse which can bring about balance in our lives. Humans seem to need to express their inner life, to share their inner life and to make sense of their inner life through creativity (Gordon 1975).

Creativity is present in many different forms. We may perceive creativity as an organic, flowing, spontaneous, interactive responsiveness which expresses itself in diverse contexts and through diverse media. Creativity is stimulated by the pulse of life through our veins: by the very fact that we are breathing living beings. In humans this sensing and feeling seems to transmute into culture of various kinds (Dissanayake 1997).

Creativity and the body

There is a strong emphasis in our book on the inclusion of the body and creative movement in the creative process. We feel that it is by animating the body that we tap into our innate creativity; creativity arising out of felt-sensation, out of rhythm, out of heartbeat, out of sensed connection with our environment and with others. So in this work we aim to reach deep down to the physical and creative core of the person to facilitate expression through the arts.

We argue that the creative self is indeed a core self, still present when many of our mental faculties are being worn away. When we introduce the arts into dementia care, we make a space for the creative self to come alive again, helping the person to escape from the traps of tangled thoughts. The arts can be our way back to our heart, to our feelings, to our images, to sensed relationship and to our memories of connection.

Person-centred practice and the creative arts

The creative arts fit well inside person-centred approaches and ideas because creative arts practice and person-centred practice share the same view of human nature (Innes and Hatfield 2004). They both believe in the creative potential of the human being; they both appreciate and celebrate the passionate, poetic, loving and giving parts of the person (Kitwood 1997).

Person-centred practice does what it says: it places the person in the centre, the person behind the illness, the person behind the label (Rogers 1957). Creative arts practice also places the person in the centre and sees creativity in the centre of the person no matter how afflicted and unusual their outward behaviour may seem. We suggest that creativity needs to be at the heart of all person-centred practice, because we are trying to engage with the healthy creative centre of the person, not their disease.

To be able to connect with the healthy creative part of the person, we need to relinquish the tendency to classify and categorize. I am sometimes told what I am seeing is behaviour typical of dementia. The person has become a label and is not seen anymore. Shuffling papers back and forth, sifting and piling them at random, the ex-newsagent is on automatic. Putting the chairs on the tables, so is the ex-caretaker, dusting, the ex-cleaner and chopping vegetables, the ex-homemaker/ cook. These are familiar operations to these people, performing them is comforting. They provide the structure which has disappeared with the stuff which glued memory and identity together. They are the vestiges of identity, residual in the body. It is important to re-vision our perception of these operations. Instead of dismissing them as nonsensical and tiresome, perhaps we can see them as purposeful, as necessary. Instead of letting them become our whole view of the person, we can learn to see past habitual movements and connect with the person inside.

Creative practice leads to person-centred practice. When we are creative we lose our sense of criticism, frustration and despair. When we are creative we are filled with love and acceptance. We need to reach our own creative heart to work flexibly and acceptingly with the difficult and challenging situations which dementia provokes. If we are in touch with our own spontaneity, flexibility, sense of fun and feeling, we can respond to idiosyncrasy with love.

From a judgement of nonsensical 'mad' absurd behaviour, 'pointless' repetition of speech and action, we can move to a kinder heartfelt understanding of the purpose the behaviour is serving. We can loosen the grip of impatience arising from our need for 'normality' in contact. We need to find different creative ways of keeping the connection with people with dementia. In being still and patient we can discover other ways of interacting which do not involve cognitive processing: we can connect in a different way when we sit still with awareness, when we dance and sing, or when we play together.

Creative care for dementia

I imagine that when I begin to drift away from my identity, and contact seems to be strange, distorted and weird, I will feel very frightened. Someone told me recently about a resident who woke up in the middle of the night and was hysterical because she could not remember her own name. Imagine this: I know that I am someone, I am in a body, but I don't know who I am or where I belong or who I belong to. This is clearly a terrifying experience; I am in a very lonely, bleak place, abandoned. How much worse if I am abandoned to nothing, to grey walls, to confinement inside, to monotony? How much better if I am cared for and appreciated as a lost human being, if someone continues to reach out to me with love, if I am surrounded by colour, art, music, song and dance? With all these stimuli, I have a chance of return to connection with myself and with my loved ones, even if they are just a memory. Memories of connection can warm me, though sometimes they are sad. It doesn't matter to me if I cry; at least I feel I am connected to someone, however painful this may be.

The creative arts clearly help people to be reconnected to their heartfelt memory as well as to find their present capacity for love and relationship. Sensation, emotion, imagination and memory seem to inhabit the same world. The close connection between these aspects of being has been explained by the juxtaposition of processing centres in the right hemisphere of the brain (Lewis 1993). When cognition through logic and language is impaired in the left hemisphere, the faculties processed in the right hemisphere can take precedence and provide the anchor of connection to past and present.

CREATIVE CARE AND THE CAPACITY TO PLAY

We strongly emphasize the importance of play in relationship in dementia care. Play in its broadest sense involves a creative, fun-loving attitude to life. In imaginative play we have no expectations of 'rightness'; we are open to the moment and we respond to it. We drop our tick sheets and we start to tango! We believe that there is a creative passionate person behind every implacable face. It is clearly distressing to walk into a room of people locked inside the shell of their condition. We must believe we can reach them to feel inspired in our work; through the creative arts we can make a strong connection touching the most closed of individuals.

My colleagues and I have seen people with dementia surface out of the blue from inertia to boom out heartily the lyrics of a song, or to get up and waltz around the room taking our hands. The joy of life and connection with others is still there even when appearances suggest otherwise. Just before Christmas, I heard a till-then motionless resident call out to the carol singers 'that was really awful!'; the tangy sense of humour felt refreshing and full-blooded.

In play, all emotions are acceptable, though clearly there must be ethical boundaries for safety. Aggression is often associated with dementia and staff and families need to be able to protect themselves against its impact. Again, creativity can help us here. If someone is 'being difficult' we can sing to them. Someone told me recently that the only way she could encourage their client to dress was by singing all her favourite songs. The songs formed a bond between the care worker and her client. Their relationship thrived on song. It became a relationship based on mutual adaptation, rather than coercion and compliance.

In working in dementia care we need often to let ourselves become foolish, unconventional, stop making sense. I have been thrilled to meet staff who at the drop of a hat will dress up, play the guitar, sing uproariously, dance around the room with scarves, waft a stretchy cloth in the air, or who have the capacity to sit quietly with someone without an agenda. It is this joy of the crazy and the still, this lightness of being, which is refreshing and life-promoting in the work that we do. We can play with balloons, blow bubbles, doodle, improvise. We don't have to make a finished product. By creatively and somatically being with a person we can instil a sense of safety, of physical and emotional security.

Perhaps it would be helpful if we were less demanding of ourselves and others in the work that we do; less focused on dramatic or perfect results.

Being satisfied with little things puts us in touch with our kindness, our 'good enoughness' (Winnicott 1985). Connections through creativity will probably not be Hollywood-style, they will often be simple and little. But we must not minimize this work. William Blake wrote about seeing the world in a grain of sand (cited in Malcolmson 1967). It's the little playful creative moments that count.

EMBODIMENT IN CREATIVE CARE

Often people with dementia become bewildered by verbal interactions. Can we let go of our reliance on words and take hold of people's hands instead? Somatic connection is essential in dementia care. We must not be afraid of it while conscious of the opening it gives to unethical practice. Kind and gentle intention can be clearly expressed through touch; touch is often the only way left to show someone with dementia that you mean them no harm, that you love them.

There is an ethical concern that we do not infantilize people with dementia. While holding this concern I would want to make a link between our state at birth and our state in dementia. Mahler and Furer (1968) have drawn attention to the pre-verbal baby's sensitivity to a variety of embodied signals in relation to the mothering figure. When cognition breaks down we become dependent again upon the body to pick up communication. If we recognize this process, we can use touch, movement and dance as ways of communicating love and attention.

We need to be able to evolve unconventional ways of communicating by attuning to the person with dementia in the same way that a mother or father attunes to their baby (Stern 1985). Attunement can only happen when we stop, look and listen with our whole being (Mearns and Cooper 2006; Pearmain 2001). In order to do this we need to become more aware of our responsive, expressive bodies.

When we understand the importance of non-verbal communication in dementia care, it becomes necessary to reflect upon our own relationship to our bodies and the messages we make with them. If we feel uncomfortable with physicality or self-expression we need to be prepared to examine why. Perhaps it is cultural, perhaps it is phenomenological. We need to face ourselves to expand our work. But we need to do this with compassion. Loving, expressive touch may feel too alien, too difficult. If this is so, we need to find our own way of contact. Yet still we need to keep our clients in mind. If they would benefit from touch, massage, a song or a dance, we need to examine what it is that prevents us from meeting them through these media. If we could transform our own fear of touch and self-expression, we could perhaps deepen our relationships with clients. Of course, all people with dementia do not want to be touched, to sing or to dance, and there are those who vociferously reject it! Nevertheless, many would benefit from gentle contact and creative activities. It feels important to acknowledge and respect differences between people, both clients and staff, but to remember that it is the wellbeing of the client which is paramount, and our responsibility to try to meet them where they are.

CREATIVE ARTS AND RELATIONSHIP

The creative arts can be a catalyst for the development of a therapeutic person-centred relationship. Healing relationship can be woven through the arts of movement, dance, song and music (Innes and Hatfield 2004) and becomes a creative bond for further expression and connection.

So many times a song and dance provides a breakthrough in contact. These media seem to have the capacity to wake us up to our feelings, our passions, our need to be connected to others. When the care worker and the resident move together or sing together a bond is made which is often felt to be deeper than cognitive exchange. It is as if singing and dancing help us to dive down beneath the surface of the frozen lake and pull out the aliveness which is still there. The song and the dance reawaken visual, musical and kinesthetic potential, bringing a person back into creative community, giving them assurance that they are surrounded by people who care for them. The relationships we make in dementia care are often dependent on somatic, emotional and artistic sensitivity. When we use these modalities to make relationship we can hold someone who is in a state of cognitive confusion. In this state words can compound the problem.

SENSITIVITY TOWARDS THE INDIVIDUAL

In bringing creative arts into dementia care we always aim to be sensitive to the individual, to listen to their requests. We join our clients in their dance, witnessing first, then responding with song and dance. One client loved to go dancing when she was younger and was particularly fond of Strauss waltzes, so we make the opportunity for her to enjoy this dance style now. The waltz is an expression of the joyousness which was and still is in her soul. Sarah researches and sings the songs mentioned by her clients, and they join in with conviction and vigour; the song really means something to them.

I do not assume that the creative arts will appeal to all people with dementia, just as I do not assume that they will appeal to all independent adults. I do believe, though, that the creative arts bring joy to many and so it is worth making the opportunity for people who no longer have the choice of going out to dances and concerts, dance classes and choirs, art classes and galleries, to bring the arts into the home to provide some stimulation for the heart and soul. It is always important to ask clients what they feel. If someone says 'go away!', I go away, and if someone says 'sing it again', I do. If someone says 'I feel better now' this is surely evidence that the creative arts are contributing to their wellbeing.

HUMAN SOLIDARITY

As I left a home the other day, Rosie said to me 'Can you take me where you're going?' She squeezed my hand and looked deep into my eyes. I believe we both knew that I couldn't, but we shared the human need for contact in that moment. As I packed up my car Sally opened her bedroom window and called out to me, 'Do you need me?' I said, 'I don't need help right now, thanks. I'm almost packed up.' Perhaps Sally was in the comfort of a past situation, perhaps she was in the present. All I knew was the power of her words. We all need to be needed. I believe that is why we work in the caring professions. That is why we must meet the challenge of finding ways for people with dementia to feel needed too. So many care staff have spoken to me about the pleasure they take in the characters of the people they care for; we can make more creative opportunities for them to share who they are, to be important, to be needed.

People with dementia and their families and friends

I wanted to include in our book the families, the husbands, wives, partners, children and grandchildren of people with dementia. Chapter 6 is devoted to you. It is hard to witness your loved one changing, perhaps no longer recognizing you, fading away from the person you once knew. How to come to terms with such loss?

Creativity can play a part in this process. Creative arts groups for families provide the opportunity for self-expression and reconciliation. Creative images, movement and songs can contain divergent and contradictory emotions, and can offer new possibilities for relationship with a changed person. Jung wrote about a 'transcendent function' occurring in active imagination (Chodorow 1997), which produces a third image from conflicting opposites. We may feel many contradictory emotions in relation to our loved one who has dementia. Engagement with the creative arts may help healing symbols of reconciliation between opposites to emerge.

I suggest that grief, anger and guilt fully felt and expressed and therefore fully in awareness, can become 'compost' for psychic growth and can help us to develop congruent interaction with the person with dementia. Holding on to feelings can increase our suffering; it can lead to resentment and inflexibility. Expressing feelings helps us to be released from them, so that we can make lighter, loving contact in the here and now.

In summary

The creative arts in dementia care can promote animation, freedom and contact amongst people with dementia, their staff, and their families and friends. This is because the creative arts can open up our hearts; they let feelings be felt and expressed, even when our verbal communication is limited, confused or non-existent. People with dementia often seem to be imprisoned on an island, with so much distance between us and them. The creative arts can act as a bridge across the water, keeping contact with the person with dementia when other bridges are collapsing.

Creativity: An Essential Energy

When we are creative we act with purity and with vitality (Winnicott 1985). Something from deep inside us pours out, unfiltered by culturally influenced self-consciousness. We make contact with something *essential* in our being. From this point of contact in ourselves we reach out to the *essential* in others, nurturing deep living relationship with them. Mearns and Cooper (2006, p.120) write about perceiving the 'red thread' in others, which I love as a symbol of heart and essence. When we are creative we are in touch with this red thread and we let it be seen.

Creativity manifests in many ways. Here we are concerned with people's artistic expression as 'a deep human cry that lies buried and unknown far below the surface of the person' (Rogers 2010). By facilitating creative expression through dance, singing, image and story, we are encouraging the 'red thread' to have a physical and tangible presence here and now. This can increase our wellbeing as emotional tensions and emergent images are perceived and released.

While we can clearly see that when dementia has taken hold of the person they are no longer who they once were, we can still catch glimpses of a creative spirit. D.H. Lawrence gives us an image for this creative spirit still thriving strangely amidst physical decay:

> odd, wintry flowers upon the withered stem, yet new, strange flowers
> such as my life has not brought forth before, new blossoms of me.
> (Lawrence 1963, p.133)

It is most important we realize that creativity has something to tell us. It has something to say about our inner life. Anna Halprin (1995) and Daria

Halprin (2003) focus upon what they refer to as a 'Life Art' connection. Art is perceived as having a link with our lives past, present and future. Art may reveal personal thoughts and feelings: 'configurations of self' (Mearns and Cooper 2006). It is possible too that art may reveal deeper patterns of destiny (Woodman 1993) which show a greater story as we near the threshold of life and death.

How does creativity relate to dementia? I am suggesting that the creative arts make three distinct contributions to the wellbeing of people with dementia and those around them. First, the creative arts provide a most necessary vehicle for the self, isolated by forgotten language, to step back in contact with life. Second, the creative arts form a relational bridge between people with dementia and those who care for them; that they aid communication and understanding. Finally, that the creative arts contribute to healing, to making whole through both of the above and through profound reunion with spirit (Boxhall 1999). I would like to expand on each one of these potential contributions in turn.

The creative arts as vehicles for self

Often it seems that the person with dementia is gone, that the body is there but the person has vanished. This perception is a fallacy and this state is often induced by environments which are draining of life energy, grey not colourful, silent not singing, sparse not rich in stimulation, devoid of hope, empty of feeling. Particularly in the state of confusion and withdrawal which characterizes dementia, it is even more essential to fill our homes, day centres and hospitals with art, with colour, expressing hope and love.

It is clear that as able, independent adults we can create art to express our feelings and perceptions, to make sense of them, to communicate them so that they may receive validation. Sometimes we create art to explore and express our links with something beyond the human, however we define it (Gordon 1975). I argue that all of these things are true for the person with dementia, though we may not be able to see it due to our own limitations. I argue that while the cognitive and linguistic computing brain is atrophying, the visual, the kinesthetic and the musical faculties may still be robust in dementia, and that it is these faculties which express our essential humanity. The talking personality may well have disappeared but the essence of the person is still there.

People with dementia still love to sing, to dance, to make. So it is important that we create opportunities to sing, dance and make with them, to encourage them to participate. In Chapters 7 and 8 we write about a lively session in which both people with dementia and their staff, participate. As energy and passion build, the interaction between people grows stronger. The arts create new possibilities for communication and appreciation.

Singing, dancing and making provide opportunities for the person with dementia to tell a story. Sometimes we have found that we knew nothing about the person's love of dancing, love of art, love of poetry or song until we gave them an opportunity to express it. Beautiful, graceful movements of fingers and arms tell a story, a song releases memories of someone past, the events of a life. Through the arts, the person returns and when we join in with them, we affirm this return with joy. We also celebrate their presence now.

The creative arts as relational bridge

I am always thrilled to see people meeting in affection. When I watch people reunited at an airport or a train station the dance between them is a flurry of contact and joy. The physical–emotional connection is mutually energizing. It sounds simple but it is nonetheless wonderful to say that we all have the ability to connect at many levels with each other and therefore the ability to bring each other to life.

Relationships give confirmation of who we are and give meaning to our lives. They affirm our identity and they can affirm our inner life too. As infants we are dependent on others to acknowledge our physical needs as well as our feelings. It is through this attention that we come to believe in our own existence and in its value. We are appreciated through the eyes of another, therefore we appreciate our own life, the roles we fulfil or have fulfilled, the purpose which drives us.

We meet people at different levels; some relationships are felt as superficial and some as deeply meaningful. It is only when another has the ability to appreciate our complexity and to accept our true colours, that we feel loved for who we are. In dementia care we are constantly challenged to accept a person for who they are now. We are constantly challenged in our capacity to love.

Being with someone as they change in dementia is painful. We long for who they once were and we find it upsetting to witness them change.

It is particularly hard to accept loss of memory and vocabulary in a culture which emphasizes youth and speed in an aesthetic of physical and mental perfection. Such change is the beginning of a journey in which there is inevitable ending and parting. Again, this is particularly difficult to embrace in a culture which avoids speaking about ending; a culture in which dying and death remain unintegrated in life. We talk about decline and death with fear and rejection, rather than with awareness and acceptance. While change in dementia is often upsetting, for example if the person becomes aggressive or violent, some changes need not always be perceived negatively. Forgetting and gradual withdrawal are part of a natural cycle of life.

O'Donoghue (1999) writes about coming into acceptance of the flow of life. Dementia may be re-visioned as an essential moment in the flow of life. It is a time when active contact with the fast workaday world is relinquished, a quiet soulful time when the inner life takes precedence; an organic response to a need for repose. Yet the loss of contact with cognitive constructs frequently enforces isolation. It would be a kindness for someone still attached to active life to meet us in our world; to keep the link but to acknowledge where we are.

Creativity begins with listening and listening is an art in itself. We have to put aside our tendency to jump in, to intercept, to interpret, to alter the outcome. We have to be still, to give time for the other to emerge. We have to hold out our hand and wait with our heart wide open. This is a different state of being to the one which is promoted in our 'advanced' technological cultures, which depends upon quick interception and reaction. People with dementia are in a culture of being, not doing, and we need to be able to meet them there. This requires a sea change in the way we meet them. We can benefit from meditation, relaxation and stillness to prepare ourselves for this creative meeting.

When I slow myself down I begin to notice things which evade my attention when I'm busy. I notice my own body, I notice my heartbeat, my digestive system. If I make some little stretching movements I begin to notice my joints and muscles. I begin to notice flexibility and I begin to notice stiffness. I begin to notice the parts of my body which need attention. My throat is dry, I have a lump in my throat, my neck aches, my eyes are sore. I may begin to notice colours. My body tells me how I am. In dance movement psychotherapy we learn to read the body not only for physical messages but also for psychological ones. It is as if we reconsider the body as overlaid with the mind, the two in one. So my dry, blocked throat is a metaphor for sadness and grief, my painful neck and shoulders express my stress carrying the responsibilities I need to lay down (Halprin 2003).

As I slow down and notice myself, I begin to notice the effect of being with another. I notice how I tense up or relax in their presence. I can reflect upon the emergence of these relational feelings. Sometimes it is my own story in relation to them which stimulates my physical reaction; sometimes it is their story which activates my own feelings (Forrester 2007). Sometimes my drive towards product leaves me ill-equipped to be still, sometimes the agitation of another stimulates my own agitation. Whatever is going on, there is no doubt that we are affecting each other in invisible and often unconscious ways.

We need in the relational work of dementia care to make ourselves ready to meet our clients in calm non-reactive, creative and responsive ways. We need to clear a space to receive them. A morning relaxation and meditation can do this. There are many simple thoughts which can free us from clutter. We can imagine ourselves as a vessel, any kind which springs to mind, and imagine it empty, in a state of receptivity. If it is helpful, we can imagine ourselves emptying this vessel, physically taking out the things which are filling us up, preventing receptivity and open-hearted contact.

Creativity enhances relationship. Cultivating a creative attitude is important in all therapeutic relationships. With a creative attitude we are open to the present moment, and willing to interact with it. In a state of creativity, we are connected to our body, to our heart, and to the bodies and hearts of others. We are connected to all that surrounds us. Analysis separates us from the thing observed, creativity rejoins us with it. Buber (1996) writes about the 'I Thou' relationship as opposed to the 'I It' relationship. 'I Thou' is characterized by creativity and oneness or love. On the other hand, 'I It' is characterized by criticism and separation or dispassionate distance.

When we are involved with someone creatively our relationship with them is qualitatively different. If we compare ourselves singing with someone to performing a functional task for them, we see that the relationship is not the same. In the first example we are joined in focus and purpose; there is a relational, perhaps emotional and imaginative link. In the second example we are sliding over the life of the other, barely making relational, emotional, imaginative contact. It might be possible though to put the two examples together, so that the song enhanced the relationship in performing the functional task.

When we are singing, dancing, moving creatively, looking at pictures or making them, we enter a different world together and this creative intention binds us together. It enhances human to human contact. It lets us know that we are not alone, that someone else is prepared to connect with us on the level of the heart. Songs, dances, movement, pictures, poems, all seem to express the heart. In dementia a person's heart is asking for expression and contact.

The creative arts and healing

The creative arts have long been valued as methods of healing. It is clear that movement and dance stimulate the immune system (Hartley 2004), reduce anxiety (Payne 2006), enhance coordination (Payne 2006) and build relationship (Hayes 2004). Creativity has been said to 'cure the soul' (McNiff 2004). The image can heal by making whole, by restoring the lost parts of the psyche, bringing the pieces together. Music has the ability to soothe the troubled mind and release pent-up feelings.

Recent research in the field of arts and health (as disseminated at 'Inspiring Transformations', an international conference exploring the interaction of applied arts and health, September 2009) offers an impressive array of studies, both quantitative and qualitative, which give vivid illustration of the impact of the creative arts on wellbeing. For example, The Sidney De Haan Research Centre for Arts and Health at Canterbury Christ Church University is halfway through an eight-year research programme[1] exploring the health benefits of community singing. Some studies focus in particular on older communities and the benefits for memory recall, physical health and wellbeing. It is asserted using the primary source of participants' feedback that when we sing we breathe more fully, the body becomes invigorated and we begin to be more fully present in community. Many songs used with older populations are songs into which we can bring actions, cross-lateral actions promoting connection between right and left hemispheres of the brain. This keeps the brain functional and decelerates the process of dementia.

The creative arts are a powerful pulse of healing. The image, the song and the dance can contain everything necessary for healing. When we are

---

1   If you wish to learn more about the programme you can access their website at www. canterbury.ac.uk/centres/sidney/de-haan-research.

immersed in an arts activity we access a healing force. We often discover that the art form contains hidden parts of the psyche still longing for expression, needing to come to the surface. Expression brings about completion, wholeness and peace.

So when we find a song that brings someone to life – or a poem, a movement, a dance or a picture – we give them the opportunity for expression and for healing. We bring the song into the present moment through our own human form. As we breathe life into it we also breathe life into the memory of the person with dementia and we awaken our shared humanity.

The creative arts carry us to a place of healing. When we dance or sing or make a picture we travel to a different part of our psyche, to our heart, to our soul, and we take up residence there while we are involved with our art form. Here is a land of feelings and emotions which we legitimize through involvement. Once we are there, they present us with lost treasures or new-found ones, which can tumble out as in a dream.

When we have sung the song, moved our dance or painted our picture, we feel different, something has shifted. We are probably all aware of an art form or a particular song, poem, film, painting or dance which moves us. It takes us to deep and hidden place in our heart. It may make us feel joyful or it may make us cry. It may uplift us, or it may feel vital to our existence. It may impassion us, it may rouse us, it may make us feel angry or sad. Whatever the feeling, we sense that it is important, but we may not be able to articulate its importance in words.

Somehow we know that these excursions into our hearts are our lifeblood, that somehow without them we cease to exist. Whether we make these excursions in songs, dances, images or other art forms, we may say that the arts are ultimately all we ever have to express the depth of our humanity. So when we consider dementia and gradual fall into the abyss of memory loss, we may need the creative arts to help us in this drifting state, to anchor us to some depth in ourselves, even when we cannot remember how things fit together in the outside world of identity.

The creative arts stimulate the senses. They awaken us not only to meanings in the past but also to the sensory pleasures of the present moment. When we play a song, or bring in beautiful fragrant flowers, or perfumes, or touch hands and move together, we are awakening the senses in the here and now. We are making a space for the humanity of the person, a space in which they can be human, in contact with and appreciating the beauty which is all around us.

I think it is important that we link the creative arts with the natural world. Gardens are places of creativity. To sit in a garden, breathing in the air and the fragrance of the flowers, the grass and the trees is healing for the soul. In the garden we can perceive ourselves as part of nature, as some quiet part of ourselves joins with the energy of the garden. It is vital that people with dementia have access to a garden, a place where they can recover some dignity, where nothing is demanded of them, where they can be free from constraint.

Often a person with dementia seems more contented out of doors. Their wellbeing increases as they enjoy the energy of the garden. The flowers and the trees have a creative energy of their own which heals the passerby. Making gardens part of residential and nursing care settings seems an important component in the transformation of dementia care.

The creativity which abounds in the garden affects the soul. Flowers, shrubs and trees may be chosen for their colour, their fragrance and the time of year they blossom and yield fruit. Often people in institutions are deprived of sensory stimulation. Lives become grey and monotone like the walls of a building. If we bring nature into the residential home we bring life back to the people inside. The garden can transform the lives of people with dementia, either as a place of sanctuary or as a stimulus for creative arts activities.

We sometimes forget that people with dementia need contact with beauty. Our senses give us our connection with the beauty of the sensory world. It is a pleasure to feel the breeze on our skin, the coolness of water, the softness of silk. It is a pleasure to see the bright and subtle colours of fabrics and costumes, and the rainbows in bubbles. It is a pleasure to hear the sound of a flute or a guitar and a pleasure to smell the scent of flowers and essential oils. It is important that we spend time finding out which senses can be awakened in the person with dementia and how. Each person will have a different response to each stimulus. But there will be something beautiful which belongs in the soul of each individual.

We can borrow from nature in our use of the creative arts. We can take ideas like a bee collects pollen. We can bring in the elements of nature. The solid, malleable quality of earth can be transmuted into work with clay, dough, fabrics or sand. Whatever substance is chosen, there will be associations as well as present responses to it. Both the touch and the smell of the substance are stimulating. Begin the work with no expectations, simply as a chance for play and awakening. If memories appear let them flow out, and listen. There may be an associated song, a dance or a picture which can be brought in now or another time. Each response is a clue for communication with the person with dementia.

The fluid quality of water can be borrowed in work with music and movement. There are voices and instruments which flow like water and act as stimuli for flowing movements. We can make gentle flowing movements, reaching forwards imagining ourselves touching the water of a lake, then reaching to each side and reaching upwards. These little gentle movements give some flexibility to the body which can become rigid sitting in a chair. Using imagination with images of nature can stir the heart and encourage some expression.

In letting the images of nature permeate our creativity we can be nourished by nature herself. We can feel peace in the presence of nature and recreate this peaceful connection through the creative arts. In a state of confusion or agitation creativity inspired by nature can calm us and give us a feeling of oneness.

Setting our creativity free

To be able to work in a creative way with people with dementia we first have to free our own creativity. If we feel shy or inhibited we need to find ways of working through this restriction. Usually we doubt our creativity because we doubt our own ability to create something which will be approved of by others. Our creativity is overshadowed by a fear of disapproval.

Little children are all creative. The cropping of this innate creativity is connected to our upbringing and our schooling as both affect our self-confidence. Certainly, we all have different creative abilities and ultimately creativity simply means making a mark, making *our* mark on life in our own way. Here though we are writing about the creative *arts*. Some people will feel an affinity with them and others will not. Sometimes, though, there are people who used to love self-expression through the arts but have turned away from them because they have been told that they are no good at them. When this happens, a great source of joy and connection with others is lost.

We would like to encourage all of you who work with people with dementia to find your taste for the creative arts again, because they can become a vital way of connecting with the person who suffers from the condition. It breaks through the fog of cognitive confusion and creates a beam of light to the heart of the person again.

There are courses we can take to set our creativity free again, whatever form attracts us. Essentially, though, we need to try to let go of the critical voice in our heads which prevents our creativity from emerging. But if we really feel that we are blocked in some art forms, then it is best to start with the ones in which we feel more at ease.

We can begin at home, playing music and dancing, drawing, sketching, painting. We can give ourselves a creative hour each day in which to fill a page with colour or with poetry, to make something out of clay, to make a puppet or a doll out of scraps of material, to make a collage out of things we have collected on the beach or in the woods. Cameron (1995) has written a very accessible book which can motivate even the most disillusioned creator into creative activity again. When we give ourselves this creative hour, we can notice how creativity affects us.

The chances are that it will alter the way we feel. It may even have a profound effect upon us. We may play, with no product created, or we may make something which surprises us or challenges our thinking like a dream. Jung wrote, 'Art is a kind of innate drive that seizes a human being and makes him its instrument' (Jung 1979, p.101). Sometimes fantastical images appear, or images appear together in strange mysterious combinations. Jung (1979, p.101) explains the strangeness of images in terms of destiny: 'The artist is not a person endowed with free will... but one who allows art to realize its purposes through him.' Certainly, imagination seems to be a faculty distinct and different from the logical, methodical brain, giving us a fresh image of the heartfelt world.

Jung would say that imagination rejoins us to the collective unconscious, a deep stratum of the human psyche, containing diverse archetypes which when reconciled and accepted create a mandala of wholeness and healing. In other words, all the contradictory energies, tendencies, potentialities of humanity must be admitted and allowed to come to a place of honesty and equilibrium. Sometimes we access sides of ourselves through the arts, which we cannot allow in our conscious minds. The arts help us towards a state of balance or rejoining. Jung would say they help us along the path towards individuation or alchemically towards 'coniunctio', the ultimate union created by the melding together of opposites.

If some music calls us and we find that we want to move or if we are intrigued by an image and would like to draw it, it is possible that the arts are beginning to awaken us, beginning to move us into creative action. Jung's reference (1979, p.101) to creative inspiration implies that we need to give up control when we are creative, that we need to wait to be moved (Whitehouse 1999). It is important to find this creative flow; it is a state of not knowing, of not being in control, of adventure.

In this state we let imagination take the lead. It can sweep us into memories, into feelings, into stories. Our memories, feelings and stories are richly nourishing for our inner life because they give new meanings to our experiences. They help us to revisit times past and they give us a fully textured image of who we are now in all our complexity. If we can give ourselves these creative arts opportunities, we become more equipped to facilitate creative opportunities for others because we know for ourselves the rewards of creativity.

The place we choose for our creativity is important; metaphorically, the place we give to creativity in our lives and physically the location for our creativity. We may not feel like being creative in a dull room with no fresh air. We may want a special place, which has colour, texture, sound and light. We can notice how we feel in different environments and we can reflect on the location of creativity in the dementia care setting in which we work. Even if we are restricted in the location we can choose, either for ourselves or for the people with dementia, we can still do something to make the location more conducive to creative activity. We can bring in colour, bring in musical instruments, things to touch and play with. People with dementia will be more likely to awaken to creativity where the setting invites it.

It may feel daunting to a lone member of staff to bring creativity into a dementia care setting. It is important that staff have creative opportunities *together* as a team, so that creativity grows in community. It is fun to dance together, to sing together, to make things together, to tell each other our stories through collage or movement.

A key finding in the Skills for Care dementia project, in which we were involved, was that staff benefited from group training in the creative arts. Joint practice stimulated and enhanced individual creativity. Individuals need to feel that their creativity is perceived, accepted and enjoyed by others. When we feel this, our belief in our own creativity grows. We begin to act creatively in the knowledge that it will be well received and that it can even make others feel good.

It is important to have a witness for our creativity. When a witness is present we feel more confident that our creativity is something we can 'go public' with. When we experience the benefits of creativity as a team, we commit ourselves as a team to creativity at work. In all the residential and nursing care settings where the project took place, the staff resoundingly fed back that through creativity they could work together more cohesively, more empathically and, therefore, more effectively as a team. They felt they could initiate more creative ideas as a group, beginning with the same understanding and intention, which had evolved through experiencing creativity together.

We need others to set our creativity alight. In a group the creative energy grows as we witness and enjoy each other's creative contributions. When a staff group has this energizing experience they are more able to take the creative ideas and approaches into the workplace. Creativity enables us to see others in a new light. For example, we may have been unconsciously undermining or dismissing the work of our colleague due to prejudices which have been hiding from our awareness. When we work creatively with another it is hard to keep these prejudices in place because creativity does not let us rest in fixed positions. Creativity helps us to turn things upside down, to see things in a different way, through different lenses. When we are playing with scarves and stretchy materials, when we are witnessing someone talk about a postcard they have chosen to represent their childhood, we cannot stay in a position of judgement for long. Creativity helps us to move towards a person, rather than staying at a distance. This closeness allows us to meet the person in their own truth. Then we begin to work with them, rather than against them and we work together more freely, less critically.

In work with people with dementia, it is unhelpful for a staff group to be distant and separate. In care work we need a staff group to feel that they care for each other, that they are 'in this together'. When individuals feel that they are part of a team that cares for and accepts each other, there will be a 'cascade effect' in the work which takes place with the residents. There will be coherence in the institution. Care and compassion will be present throughout all relationships.

Dementia care is not about distance and coldness. It is about closeness and compassion. When someone is old, alone and distressed, they need kindness, patience and love. We need the resources as staff to be able to fulfil this need. These resources come from a care culture which appreciates and values creativity as presence and responsiveness, as well as creative arts activities. Where there is a culture of creativity supported through funding and conviction, creative responses and approaches to dementia care will grow stronger and the quality of care will be enhanced.

Creativity and complexity

Complexity is expected in creativity. People with dementia will respond in many different and unexpected ways to creative approaches and ideas. We must not think that creativity is a way of having a nice time; as something bland and pacifying. We often shy away from emotions. We think that if someone is upset it is a bad thing. We seek to take the sadness away. So we decide not to play songs or show pictures which will make people feel sad.

In creative therapeutic work (particularly in the arts therapies) all emotions are respected as important. To experience our lives we need to be able to feel a whole range of emotions. Sad emotions express the sorrow in our lives just as happy emotions express the joy. To be human is to experience both sadness and joy. We need to have an outlet for all our emotions. Expression serves a purpose. It helps us to experience the present, and the unresolved past, to let go, and to find some peace.

In his novel *The Secret Scripture* Sebastian Barry (2008, p.28) gives the reader some insight into the heart of his 100-year-old protagonist Roseanne Clear. When the psychiatrist Dr Grene suggests that she might like to walk about and put her toes in the sea, smell the roses, she cries out 'No!', then reflects 'I did not intend to cry out, but as you will see these small actions, associated in most people's minds with the ease and happiness of life, are to me still knives in my heart to think of.' Later on though, she is thinking about the apple blossom and says 'I would love to see it again. The frost could only delay the old tree, never defeat it. But who would carry me down there?' (Barry 2008, p.133).

We need to be able to accept the various and complex emotions which occur beneath the surface of the human being. In dementia, emotions are nearer the surface because the veneer of social conditioning is thin. In our lives we are often taught to hide our emotions so that we lose faith in them as true responses to our situation. In dementia, this is no longer so. Emotions may pour forth as a result of and in response to our fragile state and our confusion, or they may be triggered by a song or dance movement, a spontaneous response which may reconnect us to the past, but which is also present.

Songs, music, creative movement, dance, images and poetry, as other art forms, are able to contain, hold and express a range of emotions. The art form helps us to travel across our emotional landscape, awakening emotions and making us feel alive and present. Art has a mysterious ability to unlock our emotional life and to remember our human stories.

The creative arts can hold contradictory and opposing emotions in one form. Flamenco music moves from soft and gentle to fierce and passionate in the space of a moment. It seems to hold and affirm the many moods and colours of the human heart. It seems to acknowledge the complexity and volatility of the human soul.

Sometimes we can call upon particular songs or movements to suit our mood of the moment, or the memory we wish to evoke. We can learn to notice our moods and to let ourselves experience our feelings through the arts. Then we can do the same for the people we care for. We need to be attuned to the person with dementia to sense their emotional state, so that we can meet their mood with the right creative response.

Barry (2008, p.134) writes, 'No-one has the monopoly on truth.' Each person has his or her own truth, own story, own emotions. The arts provide an outlet for these truths and do not try to make them permanent or to interpret them or to stamp them with a moral label. The arts simply allow expression without judgement. They are generous and accepting. The arts help us to become this way too.

The arts help us to tell and to appreciate the truth as we feel it now. They convey messages from the heart. The arts are like messengers, bringing us presents of our feelings. We can appreciate the gifts they bring, because they remind us of what matters in our lives, the important, deep down, meaningful things.

Here is another reason why creativity may be described as an *essential* energy. As stated in the introduction to this chapter, it carries us to the core of our being, our *essence*, and this is *essential* to our healing, to our need for contact with our inner life where experience is given meaning.

Barry (2008, p.120) writes that there are 'many strange fruits in the cornucopia of grief', and even though dementia is a condition in which the pain of grief may be perceived and felt, there are perhaps also some strange and beautiful fruits which may be found there.

2

Meditation and the Body: Depth Connection

Why is the body important in dementia care?

In this chapter I consider the body and its expressive movement as fundamentally important in dementia care. I reflect upon the body in time, the body in space, the body in the present moment, particularly noticing the body in relationship. I propose that in dementia care the creative body becomes the primary instrument of expression and relationship. I also propose that to lubricate, liberate and inspire this expressive relational instrument, we need to use the essential oils of meditation and playfulness in our daily practice.

When language goes, the body is still speaking, telling us something. Even though no words are spoken, the lips are moving. The movement of the lips expresses a truth which we need to learn how to hear, and meditation can help us to perceive this unspoken language of the body. After my reflections on time, space and the present moment, I offer some practical examples of meditative and playful ways in which we can attune our own bodies to the expressive bodies of people with dementia, and ways in which we can affirm their existence and their creativity through our embodied responses.

In my reflections on meditation and the body I draw upon the practice of cranio-sacral therapy as this discipline formed part of my continuing professional development as a dance movement psychotherapist. I believe that the heightened sensitivity to the life of the body afforded by cranio-sacral therapy could become a vital tool in all therapeutic work and that the simplicity of its method, as referenced in this book and as taught by Mike Boxhall (1999), makes it accessible to anyone who is prepared to put their faith in the body as interrelational, intelligent and wise.

The body as place of connection and healing

The body is our anchor in life. It is our touchstone of existence. Through our bodies we experience the world (Hayes 2007) and we sense our connection to the world. In dementia the body is still our anchor, though we do not have the beauty and control which blessed our youth. We still sense the world through our bodies. We are still flesh and blood. It is important that we respect the body in dementia; that we care for the body in a sensitive way. We may think a person cannot hear us, or even feel us, but we may be wrong in this assumption. The body has an intelligence all of its own and perceives and responds even though the voice of memory and identity may be unable to communicate.

In cranio-sacral therapy the practitioner learns to still the body and mind so that connection with the pulse in the cranio-sacral fluid can be perceived. This is sensed as a deep inner tide connecting a person to all creation. When the practitioner connects to this pulse, a fulcrum for healing is made. It is as if the connection allows the healing rhythm to do its work; as if the joint practice between practitioner and patient invites the pulse to swathe the body in healing.

Something similar can occur in our day-to-day interactions within dementia care if we still our minds and bodies and concentrate on being with the person we are caring for. Instead of being busy, instead of rushing, we can simply sit and be with the person in stillness. This can bring about a depth connection, a joint practice as described above.

A meditative state of mind is one in which we are *being with* the mystery of the human being. It is different from a 'calculative' state of mind (Silverton 2009), which perceives the world and the people in it as things apart, to be manipulated through objective, non-relational intervention. When we reach a meditative state, we make a space inside ourselves for both our own and the other's authentic experience. We affirm physical sensation, emotion, imagination and thought without seeking change; it is a state of acceptance.

Strangely, once we notice and accept things as they are, we then make room for other possibilities to grow organically. By cultivating a meditative state of mind in our relationships with people with dementia, we can listen to their present reality and we can respond with creativity.

The experience of the body in time

In dementia we lose our sense of clock time. We can no longer locate ourselves on the sequential time line of our human life. We are no longer part of a chronological system. Our sequential thinking is damaged and we can no longer easily participate in conversation relating to shared events. Participation in life seems threatened because we cannot orient ourselves in time.

This experience must be a very frightening one initially, when some traces to our life in chronological time remain. Most of us take comfort from sequential memory. Locating moments from our lives in time and gathering these memories around us, gives us our sense of identity and value. It helps us to construct our lives as a rational progression of events, which creates purpose and meaning. When memory is shaky, we feel shaky; like we are whirling away from our security, from reality shared with others, from a sense of purpose and direction. And so we lose hold of the present, we lose hold of the past and the future in shared chronological time.

We may imagine that in dementia, time past, present and future blur together like watercolours washed in the rain. Sebastian Barry (2008, p.210) writes in the voice of Roseanne Clear: 'Everything is always there, still unfolding, still happening. The past, the present, and the future, in the noggin eternally, like brushes, combs and ribbons in a handbag.' This image is helpful in understanding dementia. The memories of a person with dementia may still be present like 'brushes, combs and ribbons in a handbag', but they are not laid out in order anymore, they are wrapped up together. Somehow when we engage in the arts, we stir the wrapped-up memories, and feelings are reawakened. If this happens, the person is given a light in the dark passageway of confusion; they can share their memory and they can join in again.

Yet we may feel that as witnesses to memory loss, we need to cultivate a different relationship with time in order to stay in contact with people with dementia. There is a way of perceiving ourselves in time, which is not dependent upon its measurement, and which can be helpful in this reconnection. When we attune our awareness to the rhythm of our hearts and of our breath, we drop into another time world, which is deeper than human memory. We attune ourselves to an eternal pulse of life. When we do this we create the possibility of depth connection. For in dementia our heartbeat remains when linear time frames have disappeared. Our breath continues when memory has gone. The tidal movement of the cranio-sacral fluid still washes back and forth, when we are no longer conscious of our human history. By quietly attending to our own body rhythms and those of the person with dementia, we are meeting them in a different place beyond the stories of this life.

In relation to time, therefore, we might suggest that meditative embodiment helps us to attune ourselves to a fundamental and present pulse of life, while engagement in the creative arts will often blow life on the flickering of memory, so that a person can be warmed by the passion and meaning hidden in the heart of the past.

The experience of the body in space

With confusion of thought and memory comes spatial distortion. People with dementia may misperceive space and the people who inhabit the space around them. There may be a misinterpretation of physical action in their vicinity. With this in mind we need to take great care with the movements we make near to people with dementia and particularly when we make contact with them. In cultivating a greater awareness of our physical self and the movements we make we become more sensitive towards the people we move around and whom we may touch. Gentle, sensitive movements in relation to others convey a message of love, respect and acceptance. Such movements help to create security in a distorted spatial world. Intention is perceived by intuition, which is different to visual perception. This is why the internal intention of an action can soothe even when visual clues cause alarm.

The body speaks an ancient language which lies deeper than talk. Through the body we can connect deeply with each other. Through the body we can identify with another, make contact and develop our empathic awareness. Kinesthetic empathy is embedded in us; it could be said that it is part of our animal nature. Animals such as tigers and apes reach out to each other with their bodies to make contact and make movements in unison, mirroring and echoing each other, which seem to express sensitivity and oneness with the other. Humans clearly have this kinesthetic empathic potential too, but we often disregard it and repress it as an inferior function. The truth is, however, that it is an essential function in the healing of human beings who are lonely, frightened or in pain. By letting ourselves be with another through our bodies we open up a channel of connection and thereby the possibility of security through our physical and emotional presence. We hold out our hand. We say that you are not alone and that all human beings suffer and have hope and love inside them.

From the security of a home that may have been known and loved for a long time, maybe for a lifetime, people with dementia are taken to live in a new 'home' which they do not know. All is spatially unfamiliar, compounding the disorientation in space and creating further anxiety. It is important that we appreciate the possible repercussive psychological processes of the person with dementia; that we imagine what it might be like to be them. It is beneficial to us as people working with those with dementia to walk in their shoes a little. What might it be like to see things in a warped way, perhaps to hear things in a distorted way, then to be transported from a place where our sixth sense was saving us, giving us some sense of security, to the four walls of an unknown room, in an unknown home with corridors and lounges full of strange unfamiliar people? In such circumstances might 'challenging behaviour' be simply an expression of uneasiness, a plea for reassurance? Creating spatial security must be a priority in dementia care and working with the body can promote spatial security, first through strengthening the person's spatial awareness with movement and dance, and second through strengthening the physical relational bond with the care staff.

It is important to be aware of the kinesphere of the person with dementia. Our kinesphere is the personal space which we like to imagine all around our bodies, like a bubble keeping us safe from the intrusions of the world. Everyone's kinesphere is different. For some it is big and for others it is small. Some of us are happy for others to reach into our kinesphere, and some of us would not want this at all. By being with people with dementia when they are moving together in a dance session we can perceive their needs for their own personal space and we can interact more sensitively with them, respecting their need for distance or proximity.

Accompanying people with dementia as they go through their day in the home can offer valuable insight. Imagining and sensing ourselves as them, what is our day like? By being still and using our capacity for kinesthetic empathy we begin to appreciate how they physically perceive and react to their environment. Instead of judging, criticizing or requiring conformity or obedience, we begin to know what it is like for them, to understand their daily existence.

Clearly, in their own rooms people with dementia need to be surrounded with things which are familiar, things which comfort the soul. It does not matter what familiar things are chosen by the person or intuitively selected by family and friends; their importance lies in their ability to comfort the person with dementia. If the objects fulfilling this function are soft toys, no matter; it is irrelevant to say that soft toys infantilize an adult if the soft toys are making them feel better, more secure.

It is important to note where the person with dementia likes to sit and to support their choice. If someone insists upon sitting somewhere in particular we need to take time to try to understand the reasons for this rather than challenging preferences and seeking to curb them. If we perceive the person with dementia as still possessing an internal awareness of their own wellbeing, then they are the best ones to know what makes them happy and contented.

Time and space now, and embodied contact

People with dementia can be very direct in their contact with people. They often say things which are honest, heartfelt and profound. They seem unencumbered by the thoughts of appropriateness which obscure human communication in the 'people behaving well' world. This is refreshing.

We may be told that we are beautiful, that we are loved; we may be told to 'get lost'. People with dementia possess an unselfconscious ability to 'say it like it is'. It is an ability which is very 'here and now', very responsive to their feelings in the present moment.

As workers in the field of dementia care we need to cultivate our own ability to be fully present and expressive. It is by being 'awake' and open that we create connections. Presence is a great gift; it shows a determination to make contact; it is an offer of relationship.

When we are present, we are nowhere else but with the living, breathing, expressive person in our midst. We are completely attentive to this person and we bring ourselves into relationship with them. When we offer ourselves in this way, we show that we value the other. In a state of presence we encourage life to express itself. We welcome the being of the other into the space between us. We invite them to unfold and express themselves. We communicate that we know it may feel difficult, that it may feel impossible, but that we want to give time to them to listen and to receive.

This is a powerful message and is given simply by being present. To stay and wait in tremulous anticipation is to be a midwife to expression. Attention such as this, arising from a belief in the expressive feeling life of the other, offers support and security, and forms a most necessary 'holding' of the person with dementia.

Being held is the experience of the baby in its parent's arms. It is the first offer of security. As we grow older this holding becomes metaphorical; from being held by the loving gaze of another, we move to being held by the belief that another has in us, or by the memory of the other. In dementia the holding needs to return to the present moment, again through the physical, emotional and mindful presence of another, so that it can be felt kinesthetically in the body and intuitively in the heart of the person with dementia.

Mearns and Cooper (2006, p.120) describe 'listening that "breathes in" the totality of the other' through a body which is 'alive in interaction, moving and vibrating in tandem with the client's experiencing' (Cooper 2001, p.223). As the last outpost for a person departing from their historical identity, the living body provides a final and powerful place of connection. By attending to our own bodies in communication with people with dementia we bring new possibilities for interaction at this time in their lives.

Whitton (2003, p.69) writes that humanistic practice 'is always alternative, looking at all the possibilities for being creative in response to people's pain – so it reflects the uncertainty of life. It avoids dogmatic adherence to methods and programmes for change'. Likewise, person-centred practice responds to the presence of the person in the moment with no fixed templates for care or expected results. Person-centred practice starts from the moment of being with another, 'breathing in' their bodily presence, using the senses of our own subjective body to notice the other in all their being.

Pearmain (2001) suggests that feeling or heart is the base of all relationship and all knowing. While observation and intellect can classify external objects and circumstances, placing them in historical time, feeling and heart can see into the inner life of objects and circumstances, making contact with an ultimate dimension (Thich Nhat Hanh 2009) which is whole and healthy. It is this ultimate dimension which becomes more and more important in the care of people with dementia. We are seeking to make contact with the still-healthy part of the person so we need to be able to perceive them at a deep embodied level. We can do this through our willingness to be present in our own bodies at a deep level. This can be developed through meditative practice.

Mystics, philosophers, psychotherapists and scientists find a meeting place in the 21st century. The meeting place is a belief in the presence of consciousness as an intelligence which surrounds and pours through all beings and manifestations of organic life. Consciousness is described as 'the ground of all being in which material objects exist as possibilities' (Goswami 2009, p.21). Consciousness is absolute potential. If we can without judgement be with the living being of another we allow this consciousness to manifest itself and we can respond to it; we can begin to allow new possibilities.

It is important to develop our ability to wait, to be able to appreciate the little expressive signs which a person's body may give. These signs express different levels of being. They may express personality, or deeper, they may express organic rhythms. We need to be able to 'recognize and value the storyteller' (Frank 1995, p.18). In dementia the story may seem difficult to perceive because the usual way of telling is lost. And yet with patient utilization of the tremendous potential of the body as a listening tool we can receive the messages from the inner being of the other; the seed inside the withering flower. To be able to respond to the seed we need to become more alert to the messages from the seed. We must develop confidence in our own embodied intuition, believing in this subtle ability to receive the messages from the other. Our materialistically developed societies tend to diminish and even deny the intuitive and spiritual qualities of the body. Here we suggest that the body is a form of consciousness, a living intelligence. It experiences resonance in vibration with another living body and it therefore echoes the messages from the other. If we attend to our bodies we will know the emotional experience of the other and we can respond to it.

A needful response to the anxiety of the person with dementia is that of containment. The mother of the baby and child acts as a kind of skin, holding and organizing experiences. This role is especially important when life events are uncertain. Whoever is caring for the person with dementia steps into the role of mother and uses their own body to convey warmth, love, containment and security in response to the fear perceived in the other. It is important that we convey the message that we have perceived the emotional state of the other and that we are attentive to it. If we do not manage to do this, the other may experience increased anxiety, appear uncontrollable or conversely retreat into isolation.

Another needful response to the frustration of the person with dementia is the ability to reflect back the emotional communication through the quality of our body movement and voice. Such reflection reassures the person that they have been heard, that they can still be received and respected by someone, even though they may feel uncertainty in their method of communication. We can practise mirroring the quality of another's movements, showing the other physically that an essential message has been perceived. Stern (1985) writes about this skill in relation to the social development of the baby. The mother needs to be able to mirror the baby's physical, emotional and intentional self so that the baby feels confident that she can make an impact upon the world; she is empowered. It is great to think that through attention and mirroring we will be empowering the person with dementia, showing them that they matter and that their messages are taken seriously.

Another vital response to the loneliness of the person with dementia is the ability to reach out to them from an embodied heartfelt place. Here we return to the possibilities afforded by the creative arts. A gesture or movement, an image, a song can reach inside the prison created when words break down and memory fails. These moments of being together through creativity can be moments of special connection and healing. Stern (2004) refers to these moments as 'shared feeling voyages'. They are:

> Simple and natural yet very hard to explain or even talk about. We need another language that does not exist (outside poetry)... This is paradoxical because these experiences provide the nodal moments in our life. Shared feeling voyages are one of life's most startling yet normal events, capable of altering our world step by step or in one leap. (Stern 2004, p.173)

These moments make us realize that time is in the heart; that it is the quality of time not quantity or order in time that gives life to the soul, the deep, shadowy and complex feeling life. 'Chronos' is the Greek word we use to describe the present instant as 'a moving point in time headed only towards as future' (Stern 2004, p.176). When we are in chronological time we are living life by the clock, passing through and limited by the train ticket. We cannot get off the train to enjoy the fields and woods we see fly by, but we know where we are on the track. 'Kairos', on the other hand, is the Greek word for:

> The passing moment in which something happens as the time unfolds... it is a small window of becoming and opportunity. One of the origins of the word comes from shepherds watching the stars. As the night progresses and the stars turn in the sky, they appear to rise and then fall against the horizon. The moment when a star has reached its apogee and appears to change direction from ascending to descending is its kairos. (Stern 2004, p.176)

Through the creative arts we can settle more profoundly into these moments of kairos, being with the smallest of creative flickers in the night sky and appreciating their light. Stern (2004) continues:

> When the present moment of doing something together is charged with greater affect, and a stronger kairos, so as to get elevated as a sort of peak amidst the other surrounding moves and present moments; when the something that gets done together involves a time voyage of riding vitality affects across the span of the present moment. When all these conditions are met, a nodal event occurs that can change a life. (Stern 2004, p.176)

In making space for the experience of the other in our hearts, we encourage the star of the person to rise and fall. Our open presence and willingness to enter into relationship are vital to the birth of this soulful expression. The creative arts provide media which invite openness to soul. When we participate in someone's soul journey we are also changed. This is rewarding work.

PLAYFULNESS AS FREEDOM FROM CLOCK TIME

Kairos is experienced when our spirits are given opportunity for movement and expression. In the creative arts we encourage expression through playfulness. Playfulness and mirth are light and fluid; they free us from fixity. A person with dementia may find himself or herself trapped in a state of fixity, so needs a companion who is playful to shake themselves from this state.

Playfulness may manifest itself through the body. We may perform a curtsey or a bow, we may take on a role which we feel in response to the person. We may receive a nod or a bow in return. The game and the psychological contact have begun. Spontaneous playfulness such as this can often break through a seemingly implacable exterior and create a new pathway to follow in relationship. When playing, we relate to each other differently; new possibilities emerge; other potentialities for communication appear.

Playing breathes life into most situations; it brings lightness and flow. A person who is rigid becomes more flexible; a person who is stuck begins to move again. This moving is both physical and emotional; it can be imaginative and spiritual. By stepping into a metaphoric world we awaken the soul; we welcome it onto the stage of life and give it a chance to sing. This enlivening of soul is essential in dementia care where so often the person is written off as being 'less than' someone whose identity is securely felt and communicated. The soul of the person with dementia is still present though identity is dispersed.

Practical ideas for developing meditation, embodiment and creative movement
LISTENING TO YOUR BODY
Find a quiet place to sit before beginning your work, a place where you feel well. Simply give yourself permission to sink down into your body, to let your mind *be with* your body, rather than scurrying away from it like a busy little mouse. Become a swan gliding on the water. Feel the relationship between your body and your mind.

What are you aware of? You can focus your attention on your breathing, letting your mind ride the waves of your breath. You can pass your attention to your heart, its sound, its rhythm, its movement, and from here to the movement arising in other parts of your body. Notice energy in your body; feel how it travels. Where do you feel free and light? Where do you feel restricted and heavy?

Let awareness softly land in different places, look around and be with the movement and the messages hidden there. These messages may be physical, for example 'I have a pain in my left shoulder', or they may be emotional: 'I am feeling a mixture of sadness and joy', or they may be imaginative: 'I see the image of a bird with green and purple feathers' or they may be spiritual: 'I feel myself connected to a presence greater than my personal self'.

Where you notice restriction and pain, use your breath to wash over this place. Let your breath be a means of melting frozen energy. If it feels right, you can begin to make some movements to free trapped energy, for example rolling your shoulders or swinging your arms. Just follow your body's impulse for freedom.

In starting your day in this way, you develop your capacity to trust your body as messenger. Your body will become the one who will teach you about yourself and about others. It will tell you how you are feeling and how others are feeling. It will tell you about possibility through the gift of imagination; it will help you to expand beyond the confines of your own mind. It will help you to reach out to others in a new way, unrestricted by habit and convention. It will help you to become more spontaneous and authentic in your interactions with others. It will make you more responsive to their needs.

DEVELOPING KINESTHETIC EMPATHY

Sit next to one of the people you care for. Just sit with them. Begin your practice of noticing your breathing and noticing your body. Then switch your attention to the person you are with. Notice *their* breathing, notice the movements in *their* body. Just stay with their breath, stay with *their* body, stay with their movements; accompany them. Then with all your energy summon an intention to encourage their movements, to welcome them.

Now imagine yourself as this person and begin to breathe in the way they are breathing, sit in the way they are sitting, hold yourself in the way they are holding themselves, begin to embody and express the little movements they are making. How does it feel, what do you learn about them from this embodiment? Just do this for a few minutes to experience how it feels. You are physically imagining yourself as them; you are walking in their shoes. Then separate again and come back to your own breathing, your own body. Notice your difference, but also notice what is left in your awareness of them.

NOTICING ENERGY

Developing the two practices above, first sink down into your body, then begin to sense the body of the other through kinesthetic empathy. Notice particularly where there is free energy in the body of the other and where there is blocked energy. Which parts of the body are expressive? Which parts are held down?

Now make a connection with the person you have chosen. See if they would like you to hold their hand. Ask if they would like to dance with you, sitting or standing, with music or without. Use your body to find your intuition. You have perceived this person with your body; you have an intuitive sense of their story. Now in contact with them, you can move with them a little to encourage expression of the free life in their body and you can soothe the blocked energy so that it melts a little.

Working with the free energy you can magnify the expression which the person is giving; you can exaggerate the movements and increase their flow with your own more physically able body. Working with the blocked energy you can encourage rhythmic, swinging, flowing movements to soothe and release blocked energy, pain and emotion. In this dance together you are encouraging expression and catharsis; you are welcoming the person's story in movement, through your embodied contact and response. This is a healing process. It is non-verbal, it is un-languaged *and* it is profound.

ACCEPTING HOW THINGS ARE

When dancing with someone it is important to accept yourself and the other as you are. Through the gentle body meditation described in the first exercise 'Listening to your body' we are beginning this practice of acceptance. As we dance with another, we must welcome their movements, welcome their dance. We are not here to try to change them, but to facilitate the expression of their world.

When dancing with another, have the intention of encouraging their creativity, their playfulness. We can hold a positive affirmation of their spirit in our hearts and minds as we dance. We can say, 'Emily, welcome to the dance' silently or out loud. Choose music that the person likes. We can tell that they like it because their body responds, their hands begin to clap, their toes begin to tap; there is evidence of animation somewhere in their body. Now just enjoy the dance however it turns out. Follow the body of your partner; take all your cues from them. Any little flickers of movement, mirror them and enjoy them. You are part of their creative dance, not controlling it, just enhancing a creative process which has a life of its own. Prepare to be surprised!

Moving on

From my reflections on the primacy of the body in dementia care we now turn to singing and movement in conjunction. Movement often sparks sound, and singing frequently turns into a dance. The arts can easily intertwine, so it is important to have many different arts available and accessible in your dementia care context. The recommendation is always to 'go with the flow', to listen, accept and follow the creative patterns being woven with whatever media are chosen by the person with dementia.

3

Singing: The Songs of our Hearts

A chapter by Sarah Povey, voice movement therapist

First of all, to those of you who are terrified by the thought of singing and want to quickly turn over these pages and skip this chapter, in the words of Corporal Jones of *Dad's Army* I want to say 'Don't panic!' (Perry and Croft 1968–77).

The word 'singing' comes to our ears loaded with memories and swallowed beliefs. I have met countless people who tell me when we first meet, 'I cannot sing' or 'I'm tone deaf.' They back up this belief with stories of teachers from school, who denied them access to the choir or instructed them to mime, to just mouth the words because they were 'growlers'. Not a week goes by that I don't hear this from someone and sometimes from the same person again and again. I am so enraged when I hear these stories. I am incensed at the insensitivity of teachers who have ripped away the pleasure of singing from these people's lives and, in some cases, for all of their lives. Let me tell you in the strongest way that if you are one of these people, *your teacher was wrong.*

It is my absolute fundamental belief that all of us can sing; it is innate in each one of us. To voice our emotions is a natural process. It is our fundamental right to sing out our joys in life, our frustrations in life, our anger, our grief, our laughter and our love. To sing or sound without self-consciousness or reservation is to connect with your heart, with your soul and, in so doing, your connected voice reaches out to others. Why else is there a multi-million pound music industry? It is because so many singers sing about something that we understand, that we have experienced. The emotion in their voice resonates with our own, deep within, and we are moved. In the same way, if I can give voice to something I am feeling, when I sit with someone who cannot voice it themselves, this gives them a way of connecting with and expressing how they feel. It is a joint process. The thoughts, emotions and memories are theirs. Even though I may not know the details of their experience, I will feel their emotion, and can then give voice to it on their behalf. I become a conduit.

Like me, you may have been a teenager that played the same song over and over again until it drove all the family and neighbours crazy with this endless repetition. Even so, you continue to play it because it is expressing how you feel or something you believe. It is the same for people with dementia. When they have a favourite song, they want to hear it or sing it over and over; the repetition becomes a comfort. It is important that we learn to love the repetition too. In singing with someone with no vocal ability (whether actual or imagined), I can sing for them, be a voice for them, express for them, so they can connect with the feeling that resonates with the song or sound.

In 1998–99 I trained as a voice movement therapy practitioner with Paul Newham who founded and developed creative arts therapy (Newham 1999). As part of the qualifying procedure I had to find individuals and a group to work with to practise and report on my skills and experiences. I found myself drawn to working with older people, and through the referral of a friend and colleague began practising in two homes that cared for people with dementia. As my practice developed, I found that it was songs that awakened a connection with those who had dementia. So, I developed my guitar-playing skills (which remain simple to this day) and began learning as many old songs as I could lay my hands on, and time would allow. I began with about 20 songs. Some songs were those that I particularly liked and remembered my grandfather singing. Others were traditional folk songs, such as: 'I'm Forever Blowing Bubbles' (Kellette and Kenbrovin 1919), 'Loch Lomond' (unknown circa 1841), 'English Country Garden' (unknown circa 1728) and 'Oh What a Beautiful Mornin'' (Rodgers and Hammerstein 1943). I also discovered that when I sat with one person at a time, I gained more connection with them than if I addressed a small group together. I therefore began to sit with people one at a time, and sing a song or two, watching for any reaction to the music – any response, be it the faintest humming, the small movement of a finger to the rhythm, opening their eyes, or even sometimes a smile. Occasionally there was a gesture of rejection; someone turning their head away from me, or grimacing at my sound. When this happened I would simply move away, and make a note to myself to try a different approach next time. The following is the story of my first three meetings with Faith.

Before I met Faith, the manager shared with me that Faith's late husband was a choir master, so I imagined she might be responsive to singing and music. I sat with her, said hello, introduced myself and asked if she liked to sing. She didn't respond. I asked if she minded if I sang and Faith said, 'If you like' in a tone that suggested she didn't care. I decided to try anyway, and sang a free melody in a high gentle voice, but after only a few minutes Faith said, 'Can't you go and sing somewhere else?' Her response was clear and direct. Faith looked me in the eye as she said it, clearly in the present moment with me. So I left.

A fortnight later I sat with Faith again. She greeted my presence with a lovely warm smile, and seemed to be listening as I played my guitar. I decided to sing her name and as soon as I did she immediately turned away. I had lost her. My sense was that my presence had been too 'full on' for Faith, especially as I had been singing her name; a very intimate gesture. I made a note to myself to sit near her next time we met, but looking away from her or with my back to her. When I met Faith the third time, she smiled and said hello to me when I was sitting and singing with the person next to her. I imagine she had been listening and she looked at my guitar and said, 'That's a lovely instrument.' I moved and sat on the floor at her feet, and began playing. Faith listened intently; she seemed to really enjoy the sound. I offered Faith the guitar and laid it on her lap. I demonstrated how to play and Faith explored a little with her fingers, playing the strings carefully one after the other. She looked at the whole of the guitar, moving her hand across the wood and commenting again on what a lovely instrument it was. Faith said that her father used to play. I asked her what he played, but she did not respond. A little later, she said that her husband would not believe that she had been playing a guitar, and she laughed. She said that she liked hymns so, as Faith played the strings on the guitar, I held down the chords, and sang a little of 'Amazing Grace' (Newton 1779 and Walker 1835).

In these first three meetings with Faith we were getting to know one another. On the first two occasions, I offered myself to her and she rejected me. On the third, she came to me, and our relationship began.

This is what I do in my work. I am seeking a way to be in the present moment with people who have dementia, using songs and singing as my foundation. Songs offer a place of familiarity, mutual interest and recognition. My intention is to try to make a connection with them, to find a bridge between what I see as our two worlds: my present and their own world, which only they have access to. I want to establish a safe environment in which we can be present together. Feeling safe, the person with dementia can share whatever they want to and feel a relationship, even an intimacy that they may feel with very few people.

Many carers find it difficult to allow the time to sit with people in this way, because of the demands of their practical duties. Sometimes people are afraid to sit with those who have dementia, and be with them, accepting them as they are. This is often the case with family members; it can be very distressing for them to see their mum, dad, husband or wife so very different. Often family are looking for the remnants of the person that was, the mother or lover they knew. Dementia can change people's characters dramatically and we need to find a new way of being with the one we love, a way of accepting them as they are now; seeing them with fresh eyes. People with dementia are already on another 'plane', unbounded by our beliefs about our present reality. It is *us* that need to make the shift to join *them* not expect them to return to us. We need to seek out a different perspective and be courageous enough to let go of our security in our known reality. We need to suspend our beliefs and expectations in order to meet *with* the dementia.

I believe it is essential in working with older people that we have an understanding of how life is for them. The best way is to put ourselves in their place, ideally physically. I have an idea that every nurse, every carer in a home, could spend 24 hours being a resident, allowing people to lift, change, move, toilet, feed, and care for them in every way. I don't know of anyone who has done this and I'm not sure I could do it myself. It may be too confronting to allow our colleagues to care for our every need, but even our resistance to the experience tells us something. Is it the total reliance we don't wish to experience? Is it allowing others to see our bodies? Is it having someone present when we pass urine, or open our bowels, and wipe our bottom for us? Just imagine for a moment how people feel who have to have these private, intimate actions done for them. How do they cope with that change? How do they deal with their feelings about that change? Is there anyone to support and help them through this transition? They may have been a captain of industry, a high ranking officer in the forces with men's lives dependent on their commands and decisions. They may have been teachers, professors, nurses, doctors, sportsmen and women, pilots, mothers, seamstresses, mechanics. Now their confidence, their power in their self-reliance is lost. They have to deal with their total dependence on someone else, and if that is not enough, not one person of their choice, but a multitude of people depending on the duty shifts of that day. Just stop and take time to imagine yourself in that situation. Notice the feelings that arise.

If any of you have ever been in hospital you will have some experience of this total reliance on others. My husband had cause to be in hospital on a few occasions, and he describes his experience of feeling totally helpless. He was wired up to various machines and so his movement was restricted. He said that the nurses and doctors know all that is going on inside your body, your heart rate, pulse, blood pressure, temperature and they don't always share that knowledge with you, but they have no idea what is going on in your mind. They cannot tell, nor do they ask, how you are feeling. He had a catheter, so one of life's most basic choices of when to go to the toilet was taken away from him. His body urinated constantly, the urine collecting in a bag next to his bed on display for all to see. Even the disposal of his urine was done by nurses who carefully measured it before emptying the bag. He says that when you go into hospital you need to leave your sense of privacy and dignity at the door; that is the only way to cope with this dramatic change. Yet, even now, years later as we talk about this, his voice grows quiet and his eyes fill with tears. The memory of the difficulties of that experience is still very emotive for him.

I watched a male carer once treat an old gentleman who had dementia with such dignity, when he needed to go to the toilet. The gentleman needed help walking to the toilet and help getting undressed and sitting down. All the time the carer was speaking with such tenderness and reassurance, then, when the gentleman was settled, the carer came out of the toilet, pushed the door closed, and waited outside. My heart warmed to this sensitivity and respectfulness to the old gentleman, giving him his privacy and dignity even in his demented confusion.

In 2008 I read Richard Hammond's book, *On the Edge: My Story* which was published following his near-fatal jet car crash which left him with brain damage. Richard talks about his recovery and I was struck by his description of his experience of confusion:

> I shall never forget the days of struggling in what was a clinically confused state. I shall always try to hold on to the memory of

how hard it was to make sense of the world, to interact, to process thoughts and to see myself in the context of the rest of the world. It made me horribly self-centred; childish, like a toddler who cannot comprehend that there can be a will in the world other than their own. My universe centred around me and so did that of everyone else around me. I shall try to keep these memories close, because it will forever change the way I deal with other people who, for whatever reason, are likewise clinically confused. It was not always terrifying; I was not in a constant state of dejection or horror. Sometimes it was doubtless rather pleasant to bounce along, wondering what was for lunch when I had only ordered it five minutes earlier, and wondering if Mindy [*his wife*] would come back and we could see everyone else at the party I thought we were at [*he was in hospital*].The distress arising from my condition was, sadly, to be felt by the people closest to me. It is far harder, I am sure, to visit someone you know and love, and see them in such a confused state for weeks on end than it is to be the one happily asking where the bar is in a hospital ward. But in those flashes of insight and awareness, there were some deeply frightening moments and my heart goes out to anyone now similarly afflicted and for whom the prognosis might not, perhaps, be so bright as mine proved to be. (Hammond 2007, p.226)

Take time to imagine being in the situation of the person you care for. How would you wish to be treated if you were them and carry this awareness with you in all that you do?

One thing I observe that really makes my hackles rise is when people move those in wheelchairs without warning them. I have seen this done by nurses, carers and even relatives. It is as though the person in the wheelchair is a piece of furniture: 'They're in my way I'll just move them for my convenience'. What is worse is that many older people in wheelchairs have got used to this, so make no objection. Their spirit to stand up for themselves has gradually been eroded, their strength of character worn down. For those with dementia, sudden movements are confusing, even frightening. How long does it take to say, 'Flo, I'm just going to move you a little so I can bring Anna through' or 'Eddie, it's lunchtime now, let's go through.' Of course, many of you reading this may think that it is blatantly obvious and that's my point, it is an obvious courtesy so why isn't everyone doing it? In today's society if an able-bodied person were to push another able-bodied person out of their way, it might end up in a fight! Such is the strength of feeling about being moved without our own volition. We need to see older people, really *see* them as individuals, with lives, loves, joys, sorrows and an abundance of experience. They are humans, the same as us, just older and more vulnerable.

Getting practical: let's get down to it!

So, you are going to sing, and sing with other people, not entirely in public, but with others around you. This may bring up many feelings for you. You may feel confident with your voice and look forward to sharing with those you care for in this way. However, many more of you, I suspect, will feel some fear, anxiety or perhaps a clear decision that there is no way on earth that you are going to do this! Bear with me because you can if you really want to and the rewards of doing so can be exquisite.

If you don't feel comfortable with your singing voice, take time to explore your voice more. Find a place where you feel more at ease to make more noise: in your car, having a shower, in the bath. Try making different sounds. How high can you sing? How low? How many animal noises can you make? Expel air through your closed, loose, relaxed lips: This is great for loosening the muscles around your mouth. Yawn lots – great for opening the windpipe and expanding the soft palette getting ready for singing. Find a song that you really enjoy and then sing it. Don't try to sound like the singer that you know sings the song. Maybe don't sing it in the same pitch as the recording: sing it higher or lower, play with it, change the words, and sing it in your own style. It is not the quality of your singing that is important when singing with people who have dementia; it is the connection you are making. You are establishing a relationship, sharing the same moment through the song. This is what is important; don't miss out on it by being shy or self-conscious. As I said at the beginning of this chapter, to sing or sound without self-consciousness or reservation is to connect with your heart, with your soul. Don't worry either if the person with dementia says you sound awful, just laugh and say 'I know, let's hear you do better then,' or 'Let's sing together, we can both make a racket!'

Try singing your song in different attitudes or characters. Imagine you are a football fan, this is your team song and you are singing in the stands along with all your mates around you. Remember you have to be heard above the other team's fans singing too! Picture yourself as a young chorister, singing at evensong in Westminster Abbey, how might you sing it then? Pretend you are singing your song to lull a baby to sleep. You may even visualize yourself holding the baby and rocking them, or perhaps you have a tame cat that may oblige! Think of more songs and characters and explore them too. Try different songs and different attitudes; find the ones that touch your heart, ones that make you cry, ones that make you laugh, ones that remind you of people, times and places in your life. By all means sing along with your favourite songs as you work in the kitchen or garage, listening to the radio or CDs, but it is important that you sing away from the recordings as well, so you can find your own pitch, style and hear the sound of your own voice. If you find that a little voice of criticism pops into your head, let it go, be focused on how you feel as you sing. If your family complains, just keep singing, as seeing someone fully enjoying themselves can be infectious.

Another thing you can try, and I have heard people with dementia doing this, is to sing about what you are doing now. For example, while cooking in the kitchen you could sing, 'Here I am in the kitchen baking a cake, baking a cake, baking a cake, here I am in the kitchen baking a cake and now it's going in the oven.' Or you could be in the garden, 'Here I am in the garden planting bulbs in the rain, and I'm going to get wet, and the rain is dripping off my nose and now I have wet toes.' Anything, absolutely anything goes. The tune is free, the rhythm is free; the song is entirely yours. The more you do this, the freer your voice will become, and your confidence will grow too.

Choosing a song

Let's think about how to choose a song with those you care for. Perhaps you are thinking that you don't know any songs well. You can start by asking your residents what songs they know, and if they can sing them for you. Once one person starts a song, others might know it, and before long everyone is singing. Sing it enough times and you will get to know it too. If the residents aren't able to share in this way, notice what they respond to when some music is playing, and don't put on Radio One, or Five Live just because it suits you! Then, learn that song and sing it without the tape or radio, just one to one and see what happens. Managers could set the staff a task of each learning one song, a folk song or wartime song, though be careful as the latter are sometimes overused.

For staff from other cultures, they could introduce a song from their own country. Though many residents may not recognize the song, some may have travelled a great deal and might know about, or have been to, the country concerned. For example, I occasionally sing a folk song from Jamaica, which mentions 'ackee', a Jamaican fruit, and I show a picture of one. The song itself is rarely known by people I sing with, but I have had someone reminisce and speak about the time they were living in Jamaica and how they used the fruit in cooking. Connections like this can arise in the most unexpected ways. Even where people don't know a song, or where the song is in another language, the sentiment of the song will carry in the timbre, the tone of the voice.

Once everyone has learnt a song, the staff can teach them to one another, and before you know it, you are building a repertoire. If you have someone who can read music, and staff in homes often have such talents that are not known or not used, buy a community song book, folk song book or borrow them from the library and learn the songs together. Of course, managers have to make time in the duty rota for this, but the benefits will quickly show if followed through. It is worthwhile allocating time to developing this kind of creative work. Taking care of the quality of the psychological and inner life of your residents is as important as tendering to their physical needs. Have a song of the week or month which everyone learns and sings with residents as they get up, wash or walk to lunch together. Talk about who sang it originally, get pictures of that person, share the picture. Do they fancy them or not, if not, who? Where did they learn the song? How does the song make them feel? Which words do they like best and why? And so on. From a single song there is so much opportunity to learn more about someone and develop your relationship with them. Afterwards, share your new knowledge with the rest of the staff so they can also get to know and understand that person more.

I sing 'Cockles and Mussels' (Yorkston 1883) very often. It is the story of a fabled young woman, Molly Malone, who sells fish from a street barrow and then dies from an incurable fever. It goes like this:

> In Dublin's fair city, where girls are so pretty
> I first set my eyes on sweet Molly Malone
> As she wheeled her wheelbarrow
> Through streets broad and narrow
> Crying cockles and mussels, alive, alive oh

Alive, alive oh, alive, alive oh,
Crying, cockles and mussels, alive, alive oh

Now she was a fishmonger and sure t'was no wonder
For so were her mother and father before
And they each wheeled their barrows
Through streets broad and narrow
Crying, cockles and mussels, alive, alive oh

(Chorus)

She died of a fever and no one could save her
And that was the end of sweet Molly Malone
Now her ghost wheels her barrow
Through streets broad and narrow
Crying, cockles and mussels, alive, alive oh

(Chorus)

For some this is just a lovely familiar song to sing, but I have had different reactions to it. One lady said once, 'Poor Molly Malone' at the end of the song, empathizing with the young woman's story. I know someone who is moved to tears by the sadness and loneliness she identifies with in the song, and has done so since a child. This song was a favourite of Milly's. She often welled up with tears when I sang it, each time sharing that the song reminded her of when, as a child, she used to go out in a boat with her father and row under a bridge to pick off the cockles and mussels from underneath for the family's meal. Why did I sing it so often when I knew Milly would cry? Well, Milly always asked for the song, and though she still felt her grief for the loss of her relationship with her father who had died, she also felt delight from the fondness of this memory.

Songs can touch us deeply, resonating with an experience in our own lives. The words may reflect a past experience or how we are feeling that day. The song may have been released at a particular time in our lives, reminding us of someone or an important event. You never can foretell which songs will provoke which reactions. A good rousing rendition of 'Onward Christian Soldiers' (Baring-Gould 1865 and Sullivan 1871) has left a man in tears thinking of his mates who died in the war while he managed to survive. When I sang 'Abide with Me' (Lyte 1847 and Monk 1861) for Louise, a hymn which many people might avoid singing because it is a popular one for Christian funerals, she said afterwards that she felt peaceful and calm. A tender rendition of 'Edelweiss' (Rodgers and Hammerstein 1959) has left someone laughing because his brother used to sing it, 'hamming it up something rotten'. With older people, the chances are, the response you get will be authentic. This is especially so with those who have dementia because their capacity to pretend, and mask their true feelings, has gone. For those without dementia, it may be, that with their age and experience, they have grown comfortable with themselves, and no longer see the need to put on airs and graces for the sake of others. They want to be seen and accepted as their true selves. Find out why the response to a song is as it is. If the individual cannot tell you, see how you feel as you sit with them. Reflect their feeling in your own face, laugh with them, cry with them and as you sit with them in your compassion, take notice of the thoughts that occur in your mind.

It is so rewarding to sit with an older person with dementia and allow myself to enter into their world, to journey with them through their memories, and their fantasies, to learn about their experiences, hopes, dreams, loves, tragedies and disappointments. In this way I come to know them more, my understanding deepens and their character shines through. I let go from the 'shore of identity' (see Introduction), the identity with known language, known world, my knowledge of their situation and see where they want to take me. Sometimes they have a language all their own and I'm listening closely, open to words I recognize, such as 'sister, home', and those with phonetic similarities.

As I sit with Joe singing songs he recognizes, the lyrics that he has known well are beginning to slip away. He does not stress or panic about this, but easily replaces these words with some new words of his own, or another word I recognize. The amazing link is that these new words rhyme with the lost original. I find that many people with dementia do this, remembering how a word sounded and replacing it with something similar, keeping the rhyme. What poets they are!

While writing this chapter, I had a dream of being with some people who had dementia. These people were new to me; I didn't recognize them from my working life. The details are hazy, but I recall bantering with a gentleman, each of us making humorous comments, each trying to top the other and both of us enjoying the exchange. I remember a lady in a wheelchair drawing me to her and kissing my cheek, holding on tightly to my hand. What I remember most from the dream was my experience of delight, intimacy, love, a sense of feeling at home with all these people. I felt at ease. I felt natural. What I understand from this dream is that all we need do, when we are with people who have dementia, is to be ourselves. Speak easily and naturally as we always have with them, and be open to the humanity of us both. We are, after all, connected more closely than we may realize.

There is a deeper part of us that knows and understands far more than our conscious minds. If we allow ourselves to be open to this, our intuitive selves, and trust these instincts, we may stumble across some fascinating experiences. I had been singing with Pat for many weeks, perhaps months. He often looked at me when I was singing with others, but whenever I approached him to sing, he would scowl and turn his head away from me. Each time I went to the home, I always offered to sing with him, even though he had rejected me again and again. I felt disappointed in myself that I could not find a way to be with Pat. One day, before I approached Pat to sing, the thought came into my head to curtsey, as one might in a concert or show. I could not understand or fathom a reason for this thought; even so, I decided to follow my instinct. I walked up to Pat and curtseyed low. Pat looked at me, smiled and nodded his head. I settled down, sang through a number of songs, and to my utter amazement Pat watched me, listening, clearly enjoying the songs by a gentle nodding of his head. I was stunned.

After this discovery, each time I went to sing with Pat, I curtseyed as I approached him, and then again, at the end before I left. From this point on, Pat always allowed me to sing for him, he often smiled and sometimes even clapped at the ends of songs. I cannot be certain what difference this action of curtseying made to Pat, but it was the key to his allowing me to be with him. I wonder if in curtseying, it made my presence a performance, putting some distance between us. I became the performer, he was the audience. The idea of my being there to give a concert for Pat, may have been a less intimate scenario than my being there to visit with, and sing with him. Whatever difference this curtsey made, I am so grateful I followed my thought, even when, at the time, I did not understand its significance.

I have witnessed, on many occasions, this intuition demonstrated by those who have dementia. They know and understand far more than we may think. I arrived one day to sing with George as usual. A little earlier, I had been talking with one of the staff about possibly singing at her wedding. I greeted George as usual, began singing, and George sang along a little too. I was excited, thinking about possibly singing at another wedding, and I found my mind wondering about this, as I was singing for George. Suddenly, George said at the end of a song, 'When's the wedding?' I have to say I was dumbfounded. There was no way he could have overheard our discussion as we had been in another room. There was nothing in his room to suggest the subject of a wedding, and there had been no news of any wedding on the television that he had been watching before I arrived. I was shocked by his accurate revelation, embarrassed that I had been caught out, thinking of something else while I was with him, and completely stunned and amazed at his subconscious connection with me. I believe people with dementia are still connected with the world around them, though sometimes in ways not obvious to us.

I was humbled one day, when singing with Mary, a tender, gentle lady who was unable to move out of bed and had no discernable language or understanding. As I sang, her son arrived to visit. I chatted with him, and asked what music Mary enjoyed, as I do with family members when I meet them. As we spoke, I asked if she liked hymns. He hesitated a moment and then said, 'Well, she never used to, she was not a believer, but who knows she may have changed her mind since then.' I was so moved by his wisdom. He clearly accepted that his mother was still present, still thinking, still growing and changing as a person. He did not suggest that her life had stopped at the point at which the dementia had taken over. I remember this often with great humility. It was a good lesson for me.

Journeys

One of the things I hold close when singing and talking with people who have dementia is that whatever they say to me is true. It may not be the truth as I understand it, or their family understands it, but it is their truth. Perhaps what they are telling me is a combination of occurrences in their lives, or an expression of something about their lives now. Let me give an example. Cynthia appeared very anxious one morning, when I sat and greeted her before singing. She was looking around and out of the window. I asked how she was. 'I don't know where they are,' she said. 'Who?' I asked. 'My mother and father. They dropped me off here, and said they'd be back, but I've been waiting and waiting and they haven't come.' Now on reflection, Cynthia's behaviour could hold many explanations. It may be a memory from her childhood, when her mum and dad left her somewhere for a while, and she wasn't clear what was happening. It could have been during the war, and maybe Cynthia was evacuated, like so many children. Her mum and dad may have dropped her off, assuring her they would return, and it was not until months, or years later, that they were reunited. Perhaps Cynthia is recounting her experience of the present that she has been 'dropped off' at this nursing home, and doesn't understand why. It may be a mixture of the two, or a multitude of experiences. It really does not matter what is the factual truth. Cynthia's anxiousness and concern were actual, real, and true in that moment and she chose to share her feelings and confusion with me.

What to do in this scenario? I could tell her that what she is saying is all nonsense, and try to explain what is really happening, but to do so would negate her experience. To have tried to explain logically to Cynthia the factual truth would probably have caused her even more anxiety and confusion. By remaining with her, in her experience, I had the opportunity to learn more about her. What I decided to do was to ask her where she thought her parents were and she talked about this for a while. I suggested that I could sit with her while she waited for her mum and dad. She agreed, so, while we waited, we sang some songs and Cynthia joined in. Cynthia became absorbed in the songs, talking about them and trying to think of others we could sing. Through the songs, the experience she had been remembering and the anxiety she felt disappeared, for how long I don't know, but for the time we were together her discomfort was eased.

With situations like this I wonder if the person is reliving an experience of the past, something that connects with strong emotions, and perhaps a situation that was left unresolved. I do believe that as we near death any unresolved issues in our lives will sneak up on us again, make themselves known, and give us the opportunity to find a way to be at ease with them. Why should this be any different with people who have dementia? Without cognitive language to share what is happening, we have to find another way to help ease them through these times.

I recall another situation with Lorna who appeared very upset one day when I went to sing with her. I said to her that she seemed sad, and she told me that she had offended her father and felt terrible about it. Lorna went on to describe a situation where she had been going out for the evening, and her father had not wanted her to go in the outfit she was wearing. Sound familiar? I know it does to me. Lorna had gone out anyway, defiantly and delightedly, demonstrating her independence. When she came home later, Lorna came into the hallway, and saw her father standing on the stairs. He looked at her with such hurt and disappointment in his eyes that Lorna felt guilty, and wished she had never done it.

It took Lorna a long time to recount this story to me. She described the experience in detail, her voice stopping many times as she struggled with her feelings. She repeated herself over and over, covering her face with her hands, finding it difficult to speak. She sounded deeply regretful of her actions, ashamed of what she had done. 'I never wanted to hurt my father, I wouldn't want to do anything to hurt my father,' she said through her tears. Lorna was bereft and didn't know what to do. 'I haven't spoken to him since then,' she said, 'but I want to put things right before it's…', her voice trailed away.

The strength of her emotions at this recall of a situation happening in her youth, when Lorna is in her 90s, was astounding. Her emotions were now, real, true. She spoke and acted as though this altercation with her father had happened just last night. How did I respond? I could have chosen to put her right, to tell her this was something that happened a long time ago. I could have told her, her father is dead and so she can't speak to him anyway. Imagine how damaging that would have been, loading more confusion, grief and angst on Lorna. I chose to sit with her in her experience, just as we might a friend who is going through difficult times. I asked her what she thought she could do to resolve the situation. Lorna didn't know, her tears and shame too strong for her to think. After a while I said, 'I wonder if you could talk to your father?' Lorna considered this quietly, and then nodded, 'That's what I have to do, I'll go and tell him how sorry I am and that I didn't mean to hurt him.' She decided that she would go that evening and thanked me for my help.

With a plan to rectify the situation with her father, Lorna's mood brightened. She knew what she needed to do and she was determined to put things right. When I saw her after that, Lorna never mentioned this again. While I cannot know for certain that she resolved this issue for herself, just the fact of sharing her experience, of speaking it aloud, being heard, and witnessed without judgement, certainly helped her find some comfort in the moment. Sometimes the singing is not important. Singing with someone establishes the relationship, a closeness, a bond, a shared space of trust where openness invites and allows expression of our emotions and experiences, in whatever way we choose to express them. For Lorna, on this occasion, speaking was the more important use of her voice.

I have known people with dementia imagine they are someone else completely, perhaps taking on the character of someone they have admired in the past. For example, would you believe me if I said that I have sung with Robert Burns? Unlikely, as he died in 1796! Yet, whenever I sang a Scottish song with Fred, he would sing along robustly and then say at the end, 'I wrote that you know.' I would give a surprised smile and tell him how much I liked the song. It doesn't matter that what Fred was telling me was factually untrue, and I never corrected him, so why did he say this? My guess would be that Fred enjoyed the songs of Robert Burns, and in so admiring him, accepted the skills of this man as his own. In fact Fred was a poet, just like Joe I wrote about earlier. As the dementia progressed, the words of songs began to elude him, and so Fred added new ones which always rhymed with the original. Who knows, Fred may have written poetry in his lifetime. He had no family for me to check this out with, but he may well have done.

Helping one another

I am so often delighted by the sight of people with dementia relating to one another. In spite of their condition, their characters shine through, and the tenderness, care and concern that I witness from people with dementia often amazes me. Writing this now I wonder why. Why should I be amazed that our innate humanity and care for one another is shown and demonstrated in those with dementia? Jill wrote earlier (see Introduction) about our need to be needed, to be wanted, and I see this demonstrated in the homes I go to. Lilly is sitting next to Alice who is sitting with her head down, quiet, alone. Lilly looks at her and speaks to her. Alice doesn't reply. Lilly touches Alice's knee and speaks tenderly, then she leans forward, and kisses her on the forehead. Alice lifts her head and smiles. Lilly speaks tenderly again, smiling gently back. This delight and care for one another can also spark new relationships. A gentleman who wants to be the protector, the provider, may connect himself with a lady needing assistance to walk, or offer a guiding arm as she moves carefully to sit in a chair. Even I am shown concern for my welfare. Have I had a cup of tea? Am I warm enough? Do I need assistance carrying my bag? These people who are in some instances barely able to move, are offering their help and voicing their concern for me. Charles is unable to walk, so is confined to a chair and yet each time I pack my bags at the end of a session, he asks if I want a hand carrying them out. He is not physically able and yet his courtesy overrides the acceptance of his physical limitations, and I am touched and grateful for his attention.

It's OK to receive

This may seem an odd thing to say but it is alright if you find you are enjoying yourself as you sing with someone who has dementia. It's OK for you to show your feelings, whether you are moved to tears by a song, or are responding to the reaction of someone else. It's OK to feel like laughing aloud from enjoyment, or at the humour expressed by the person you are singing with. When I started my work singing with people who have dementia, I had the mentality that I was 'at work', and therefore all my focus had to be on giving. I was taken by surprise when I found that I was enjoying developing these relationships. I felt delighted when someone said that they liked my voice, or that my face is beautiful, or they laughed at my jokes. Then later on, I felt guilty. Surely I was not supposed to be getting something from my work, if I was receiving so much myself, perhaps I wasn't doing my work properly. Yet, true relationships are about giving and receiving, give and take, as they say, loving and being loved in return. As Jill wrote earlier (see Chapter 2), to be loved and to love another is fundamental to our existence as human beings. Gradually I realized that the more I give of myself the more I receive *and* that is alright.

People with dementia are able to be in a relationship, to give and to receive. This is natural, and it is important to acknowledge their gift to us when this happens. When someone compliments my voice for example, or admires something I'm wearing, I say 'Thank you,' and I breathe in and absorb the emotional experience, I draw in the delight that I feel. To say anything else would be to dumb down the compliment, to distract from the experience and observation of the other person, to deny, belittle or even destroy their gift. This is the case with anyone who compliments us. I learnt this through my own self-development, and though it took me time to learn to respond in this way, it is of great importance. To share your feelings truthfully with another is an enriching experience. I am being myself, which allows and encourages the other person to be themselves, and so the relationship deepens.

I'm singing a song with Marie, when suddenly I forget the words that start the next verse. I keep playing guitar as I'm thinking, then I say out loud, 'I've forgotten the words!' Marie starts laughing, I start laughing, and suddenly we are together in the moment, one another's laughter making us both laugh even more. What could be seen as a mistake, my forgetting the words, becomes a catalyst for deeper connection. This is the importance of being ourselves. We never know what might spark a connection with the person who has dementia. To trust our own process, to be natural, easy and open to all possibilities, this is the key. I have found great love through my singing work. Hilda, who has no language but appears to take in all that happens around her, reaches out to me and cups my face in her hands. June, whose eyes fill with tears at the beauty of the sound of the guitar, looks at me with tenderness in her eyes. Kenneth, who has enjoyed a lively dance with me, kisses my hand and then pulls me in for a hug. I would have to be some kind of automaton not to be moved, not only in witnessing such expression of love by someone with dementia, but to be the recipient of their outward demonstration of their love. Even acknowledging that they may be seeing someone from their past in my presence, I am the one receiving the physical expression of their memory of love. The naturalness of such an affectionate expression is beautiful. It is OK for me to feel such love.

The singing relationship

Let's imagine now being with someone you care for and how you might start a singing relationship with them.

First, make sure that you will not be interrupted for the time you have set aside for this, say 15 to 20 minutes. Turn off your mobile! If you are working, let your colleagues know that you are giving this time to 'Ruth', or whoever, so they don't disturb you. They can also help protect your space by ensuring others don't disturb you either. This is an important practice, and deserves to be honoured and respected in this way. Now, before you approach whomever you have chosen to sing with, take time to slow yourself down. Older people live life at a slower pace than most of us in modern society, so we need to slow ourselves down to meet with them where they are. This is especially true for people with dementia. Remember how Jill wrote earlier (see Chapter 2) about them having no concept of linear time. All their experiences are happening right now. Memories are often no longer occurrences in the past. The experience of the memory is relived in the present moment. For all of us, when we recall an experience from our past, the emotion we feel in response to that memory happens now, in the present. We can understand this differentiation. The person with dementia cannot.

Take time to breathe, breathe deeply, let your daily worries and demands drop away. As you breathe, feel the area of your heart expand with each breath. Become aware of the loving, caring person that you are. You have so much love, receive so much love and give so much love. Your choice to be a carer, even though it may not always feel like it, comes from your heart, from a centre of love. Whether you are an employed or a voluntary carer, you have compassion for people, and want to make a difference in their lives. You want to enhance their quality of life and yours too in the process.

Once you feel relaxed, move slowly and calmly towards the person you have chosen to sing with. Greet them by name and with a bright smile as you sit down. Lift your hand gently, and rest it on their hand, arm, knee, whichever feels most natural and within your reach. If they speak to you, look into their eyes as they speak, give them your undivided attention, and listen with your ears, eyes and heart. The individual Chinese characters that make up the verb 'to listen' (see page 6) are: 'ear, you, eyes, undivided attention and heart'. This Chinese word clearly highlights what is important if we are truly to listen to someone. It doesn't matter if you are unable to understand what they are saying, it is the quality of what they are saying that is important. As you talk and listen, become focused on this person. Take time to look at them, really see them for who they are now: the shape of their hair as it falls, the lines of experience on their face, their expression. Are they smiling, frowning, eyes closed or open, restful or alert? How are their hands positioned? How are they moving, with flowing movements or sharp jerky ones? Do you see a movement repeated? Is it a movement you recognize: mixing, sewing, hammering or tidying, perhaps? What is happening in their feet and their legs? Feel what your sense of them is. How are you feeling as you sit with this person? Are you continuing to feel relaxed, or has that changed? Be very aware of how you feel, as you may be picking up on the feelings of the person you are with.

Whenever I meet someone with dementia for the first time, I introduce myself by name and ask them theirs. This gives me an immediate clue to their cognitive ability. I explain what I am there to do, ask if they like music, and if so, what sort of music they enjoy. Do they like to sing, do they have any favourite songs and so on? I ask these questions even if someone has not responded at all. I always remember a story told to me by one manager who worked as a nurse on a ward, caring for people in comas. She recalled that when one of the patients came out of a coma, they were able to remember which staff had treated them tenderly, and which had been harsh with them. Therefore, I always presume that anyone I am singing with can understand me, whether it is obvious or not, whether I see a reaction or not.

Now you can start thinking about a song to sing. If someone already sings, then sing a song you are aware that they know. If they don't sing, think of a song they might enjoy, one that will suit their character, or mood. If you are new to singing and have just learnt a song to share, then tell them this. You might say that you have just learnt this song and are wondering if they might know it. So breathe and begin. You do not need to sing loud, projecting like a great opera singer, nor in the style of a crooner like Frank Sinatra or Bing Crosby. Sing in your own voice at a pitch and volume that feels easy for you. As you sing, watch for any responses. Their fingers or head may move to the rhythm. They may smile, hum, sing or their lips may move quietly with the words. And, if you see nothing happening outwardly, don't be disheartened that you cannot know what is happening inside; they may be soothed by the song and your presence. If you are told to go away or experience rejection in any way, then acknowledge their request and leave. That is simply what happened today. Don't give up forevermore; try again another time, perhaps with another song. Recall what I said earlier in this chapter about my first meetings with Faith. The first two occasions she did not want to know my presence, and then the third time she chose to come to me. It is my belief that those first two meetings were opening the way for the third, though on the surface they may have seemed a failure. I believe Faith knew that I was there for her, that I was open to a relationship with her, and would be each time I saw her, waiting until she felt ready to engage with me.

I choose songs in different ways. People who are able to may ask for a particular song, or may often be singing a particular song, so I remember what one they like. With others I listen carefully to what they are saying. Even though I may not understand all their words, there may be some which are clear, and so give me an idea of something to sing about: 'holiday...sister...Devon'. I will then scan my mind for a song relating to any of these, perhaps 'Summer Holiday' (Cliff Richard and The Shadows 1963), or a popular Devonshire song, 'Widdecombe Fair' (traditional song, unknown author and date). Another time I might be more focused on how someone is feeling, and so choose a song to suit their mood. If they are laughing, a comedy song like, 'Two Lovely Black Eyes' (Coborn 1886). If they seem energetic then perhaps, 'Knees Up Mother Brown' (Weston and Lee 1938). If sad and tearful I will reflect that in a song too, perhaps 'Danny Boy' (Weatherley 1913) or 'Red Sails in the Sunset' (Williams and Kennedy 1935). With regard to someone crying, your natural response may be to sing something jolly to get their mind off whatever is upsetting them. However, this is not our practice in arts-based therapies. All emotions are welcome, valid, and even when singing, it is important to sit with the person and acknowledge how they are feeling. I often find that when I sing gentle songs with those who are tearful, the sadness soon subsides, having been expressed, heard and acknowledged. Singing together, especially one to one, often brings great comfort.

In conclusion

As you venture into the world of creativity with perhaps this new way of relating to those you care for, I would like to encourage you not to be afraid of trying new things, new ideas that may occur to you. You will have your own inspirations; listen to them and try them out. If they turn out not to work as well as you hoped, adapt them. There will be some essence of your idea that is right, or you would not have thought of it. Perhaps you just need to interpret it in a different way. Most of all, if a song or idea doesn't work with someone it really doesn't matter; perhaps it will work on another day, or with someone else. The most important factor is, you are trying to make a heartfelt connection with someone who needs to feel that essential human contact. They need to feel loved, needed and wanted. They want to thrive in their older years, to still enrich themselves and delight in life, with those around them. You can help them to do this, and you will flourish in your own life too. At the end of the day, and at the end of our lives, we are all the same. Let's meet one another in the songs of our hearts.

4

Moving: The Dances of our Spirit

In this chapter I give ideas and case studies to help you to find a way of including expressive movement in the daily life of your home. It is depressing to witness, day after day, stagnation of life, people sitting lifeless, frozen in fossilized cramped positions. While clearly there is no longer the freedom of movement of youth and the body feels stiff and painful, there is still the possibility of awakening into expressive movement. Even if that movement is minimal it can still be full of meaning and expression. We are seeking to re-engage the person with dementia through movement and music, to make the opportunity for being in contact through self-expression.

Music often animates and awakens us from torpor. It reminds us of times past and brings us into the present. When music plays, we can feel a bodily response, a vibration in the cells, a stirring in the heart. It is this cellular awakening which we seek in bringing music and movement into dementia care. It constitutes a 'not giving up' on the person, a knowing that the body can still feel and express emotion even when the conceptual and verbal identity of the person is coming and going.

Will you, won't you join the dance?

Clearly it is important the people don't feel coerced into joining the dance. Being forced to take part is never going to allow expression from inside, is simply empty gesture. So it is important first that we make a welcoming environment where people can choose to take part or choose not to take part. We create an environment where there is opportunity for movement, but also the choice to be still.

We engage with the people with dementia through our own expressive movement. We seek to link with them through dance. We invite them to move with us with warmth and acceptance, suggesting possibilities for movement, little stimuli which can open the door to expression of memory and feeling. It is helpful if there is more than one facilitator to encourage these possibilities. Invite as many care staff as possible to take part. Make a circle of chairs so that everyone can see everyone else; so that there is optimum opportunity for contact. Make sure there is an empty space in the middle where people can get up and dance if they are able.

Here are some possibilities for movement and dance. Each heading can be seen as a dedicated session or can be linked together depending on the energy and concentration of the group. Throughout the movement sessions it is vital that as facilitators we are fully engaged ourselves with the music and the dancing, that we open ourselves up to being expressive and communicative; that we open or eyes and our hearts to the participants, listening to them as depicted in the Chinese symbol 'to listen'. Eye contact is essential as we lift our heads and look outwards to others. In doing this we encourage the participants to do the same.

Holding hands

Hands are the point of contact for most interactions. We reach out and push away with our hands. They are our feelers *into* the outside world and they express how we feel *towards* the outside world. So we begin with the hands as a way of making contact with the people in our movement group. The music can be chosen to match the energy, mood, musical preference and purpose of the group. Is the intention of the group to raise the energy or to calm it down, to enhance relationship, to deepen embodiment? We could choose 'flowing music' or 'rhythmic' music with a beat. Flowing music encourages sensitivity and awareness of self and others; rhythmic music wakes us up and helps us to feel ourselves inside our bodies. There are many songs about hands, and 'I Want to Hold Your Hand' (Lennon and McCartney 1963) is great for the following activity. Here is a possible sequence for the session:

1. Rubbing our hands together.
2. Shaking our hands.
3. Using our hands to smooth and pat ourselves: patting and smoothing our own arms and legs.

4. Then the facilitators move around the circle, holding and smoothing hands, beginning some movement with hands joined.

5. The important idea here is that sensitivity to the hands of another is being developed; that we are not just grabbing hold and moving in a functional way, but that we are making time for a different kind of sensitive contact.

6. We notice any energetic or movement responses, however small, in the person we are working with and we begin to mirror their movement, to join in with their expression. We are uniting with the person through our movement; we are affirming their existence.

7. We try to feel the energy and the mood behind the movement; its expressive potential. Through our own linked movement we can begin to empathize with the person and to take on the movement quality. We are affirming their expression.

8. We can be in dialogue through movement. We can respond congruently and playfully. We make a little dance together without words.

Reaching out

As we feel cut off from the world because our thinking is disjointed, we begin to withdraw into our bodies. We reach out less and less. There is a lack of safety when the mind begins to fall apart and many things no longer make sense. Through a movement session it is possible to re-establish the ability to reach out to others and to feel less confined and isolated. The psychological states which may accompany dementia, for example fear and anxiety, irritation and anger, sadness and hopelessness, can be affected by movement in interaction with others who want to make contact. Spontaneous movement without judgement creates a profound contact beyond words. It can have a physical effect, for example greater physical self-assurance, and it can have an emotional and psychological effect, for example a greater sense of wellbeing through connection with others. If practised over time it can make a considerable contribution to the physical and psychological welfare of the person with dementia.

1. Reaching up above, one arm then the other.

2. Reaching forwards.

3. Reaching to each side and reaching towards another sitting by our side, maybe touching the other.

4. Reaching, feeling the space all around us.

5. Facilitators can move in front of the person, playing with the idea of reaching towards the other from further away than in the previous exercise.

6. Look out for any expression in the person you are working with and replicate it, affirm it. You are emphasizing the quality they are giving out; you are maximizing its expressive intention.

7. Sometimes people may say what they are reaching for, what the movements remind them of. Whatever the response we can accept it and play with it; we can seek to allow its full expression. Something of the spirit of the person is being shown, something of the inner being of the person is being shared.

Two shoulders are better than one!

We take a lot of cares upon our shoulders. We talk about 'shouldering the burden', 'carrying the weight of the world upon our shoulders'. Our shoulder blades are beautiful bones, delicate, strong and large and we can indeed carry a lot with their help. It is also good to put the burden down and share it with someone else for a while, just as it feels good to let someone massage our shoulders or simply place their hands lightly upon our shoulders. We can do this for people with dementia as we can in any context of human sharing and healing. Any music to suit the mood and energy of the group is appropriate; the choice of music is stimulated by knowing the group, by an intuitive sensing of the needs and relationships in the group. 'Pack Up Your Troubles in Your Old Kit-Bag, and Smile, Smile, Smile.' (Powell and Powell 1915) is a rousing cheerful song, containing the sentiment of togetherness and solidarity, and the feeling of being able to carry the burden with a light heart, warmed by this sense of human affection. Throughout this activity try to encourage people to look up and outwards and towards each other.

1. Raising the shoulders and letting them drop.

2. Rolling the shoulders forwards and backwards.

3. Raising the arms up high and bringing them down to the knees.

4. Reaching the arms forwards with palms opened upwards (as if giving out something precious).

5. Returning the hands to the heart (as if bringing in something precious).

6. Swinging the arms forwards and backwards, possibly standing or even marching.

7. Finally crossing the hands and arms over the heart.

Taking a stand

Frequently people with dementia have lost their confidence in their own feet, in their own legs. They are dependent on others to move them around, to guide them or to wheel them. In a movement session we might focus on the feet and legs with the intention of strengthening them and giving the person a sense of contact with the floor and a sense of their own uprightness, we might say a sense of self. The song sung by Nancy Sinatra (Hazlewood 1966) 'These Boots Are Made for Walkin'' is a funny uplifting song helping us to begin to move the feet. It has a nice easy beat which people find welcoming and can respond to with clapping, stepping or stamping, or moving shoulders up and down.

1. From a sitting position we can begin to lift our feet and tap them down on the floor to the rhythm of the music.

2. We can reach each foot forwards, maybe pointing it a little.

3. We can move each foot to the side, a few times on either side. It can be fun to make these little movements together, making eye contact, smiling.

4. We might be able to stand and hold hands with a partner, stepping from one foot to the other, emphasizing each step by sinking our weight into the movement.

5. Once these little movement rituals have been made together we can begin to look out for individual responses and weave them into the dance. There are certain to be quirky little stories coming through in movement, which show the spirit of the person.

6. The trick now is to notice these little movement stories and to make them part of the movement session. It is a joyful non-verbal way of making sure everyone's presence is acknowledged, accepted and enjoyed. We can think of dance as a conversation in movement.

7. As these little dances emerge we can encourage the group to try out each person's contribution.

The dear face

People's faces are wonderful and so are their bodies. Everyone's face tells a story, as do their bodies and the way they move. It is lovely to see the story in the animated person. It is also sad and beautiful, painful and powerful. It is important to give people a chance to show their faces and the stories held inside them. We can begin this process again with movement. Christy Moore's (1989) rendition of 'The First Time Ever I Saw Your Face' (MacColl 1957) is a soft and gentle version of this beautiful song. If participants seem not to be engaged, we can move sensitively towards them to see if they respond when we reach out for their hands and make the movements with them.

1. Rubbing our hands together as in 'Holding hands' above.

2. Noticing the palms of our hands and the upper part of our hands, our fingers and our wrists.

3. Facilitators can move round the group, rubbing and smoothing hands of participants.

4. Placing our fingers on our faces, making little circles all the way around our faces.

5. Letting our necks move a little, tilting our heads forwards and back and side to side.

6. Rolling our shoulders a little.

7. Opening our eyes and looking around the group.

8. Seeing if we know the other people's names in the circle.

Action dances

There are many action dances which are popular with old and young alike. They are a way of getting people moving, stretching, reaching, holding hands, patting themselves, each other, moving their feet, even taking partners and waltzing round the room. 'We're Going to Hang Out the Washing on the Siegfried Line' (Kennedy circa 1939–40) is a good example of a song which can be sung together along with making arm and hand actions together.

It is also possible to take a song which everyone seems to know and enjoy and begin to put movements to it which everyone can follow. These movements may be gathered from the initial responses of the participants (like a choreography) or they can be suggested by the facilitator, chosen to awaken hands, arms, feet and faces as above.

Moving in unison makes us feel happy because we feel that we belong to a group. It can give us a sense of security and wellbeing, a sense of something solid anchoring us to humanity. Even if we are not actively joining in, to be part of the circle of rhythm and movement can still have a beneficial effect upon us. This likelihood is increased if we are perceived as being part of the group, having a place there, whatever our present state and contribution.

Themed dances

There are themes which bind us together as a human race. There are themes which soften us, which make us laugh, which let us be sad, which let us feel part of a group, and part of nature. When Spring comes we are more aware of nature, we are aware of the new buds and flowers, of the birds, of things deep down in the earth, moving through the earth and flying over its surface. We are aware of life, of things awakening. Just going outside into the garden we are affected by the stirrings in nature. And something awakens in *us*. This garden awakening can be brought into the movement session. We can bring nature into the movement circle, either through pictures of nature of things gathered from the garden or from walking in the countryside. A nest, a twig, some flowers, some leaves, some earth. All these things have a scent, a texture, a form, which arouse memory and desire for life. People may begin to respond to these offerings from nature with a gesture, a movement, a verbal response, a song. However small the response, we can scoop it up and include it in the movement circle. It is an important contribution. We can play songs about the Spring; there are hymns of joy like 'Morning has Broken' (Farjeon 1931) and there are songs of a different ilk, 'saucy' songs like 'Makin' Whoopee!' (Donaldson and Kahn 1928).

So we bring in catalysts for memory and expression. We watch the movements flicker in response and we include them in the dance, perhaps choosing a song that everyone likes to support and which inspires the spirit of the dance. We end up with a dance where everyone has contributed in some small way, which can be danced together for fun and because it has significance for us now.

Showtime

I seem to know many people with dementia who love a bit of show business. People who like to dress up a bit, with make-up, with hats, with scarves and who like to sing the louder showbiz numbers. 'New York, New York' (Kander and Ebb 1977) always seems to get people going. This song exudes a feeling of real joy in the moment, a sense of wellbeing in the here and now. There are many such songs which seem to revel in the moment of being in a particular place, for example 'Penny Lane' (Lennon and McCartney 1967). We can encourage people to give a movement into the circle in response to such songs, we can support people in getting up and strutting their stuff in the centre of the circle for all to see. In a way we say 'welcome to your spirit' when we encourage people to dance and move in this way. We are telling them that we appreciate who they are now.

Celebrations

We have so many wonderful celebrations and rituals in our multicultural societies. It is important to know our community of people with dementia, to find out which celebrations and rituals mean most to them. Many of our celebrations are a chance for families to be together; they are moments when our roles of grandmother, grandfather, mother, father, son, daughter, and so on, are on parade. We sink into them and enjoy them, or else we resent them and rebel against them. It is only when these roles are becoming shaky that we may feel saddened by their loss. So celebrations of family may bring up many feelings for the person with dementia. There may be the warmth of memory, the sadness of memory, a vague sense of something missing; or there may be complete absence of memory and simply the presence of now. So when we bring celebration and ritual into our work with people with dementia we must be prepared for anything to emerge. Perhaps there will be strands of memory lingering in the mind needing expression, or perhaps there will be spontaneous response to now.

CHRISTMAS

All the Christmas trappings glitter and shine; Christmas songs and carols play from the radio and CD; sherry is offered. What about the internal experience of Christmas? How do people with dementia feel surrounded by the signs of Christmas? There will be memory, there may be a sense of being part of the seasonal festivity or maybe a sense of being outside it. What we are seeking is inclusion in the celebration with an active respect for the person's individual experience.

We need first to spend time with the person to get a feel for their experience of the Christmas period. Chances are, when they had their full strength and vitality Christmas was experienced very differently to now. So this is a new time and place, a new experience with echoes of an older time. We need to meet the person with dementia where they are now in their life and take time to enter into their world with imagination, like going into a house for the first time and looking around at all the things there. We need to go there with them without seeking to pull their experience round into a more familiar shape. We can walk into the house with a sense of wonderment, with curiosity, knowing that it will not be like we are expecting, it will not conform to the models we know. A secret of dementia care is to give up trying to make the person with dementia 'fit'. They have changed; they have their own unique perception, their own unique experience. The great thing is that their essence is still there; the essence of their being.

I think that we are all longing for deeper connection with others; that we are all seeking to come out from our shells and to meet with others. Celebration is one way in which we reach out and share. So it is important that we take time to find out each person's response to Christmas and to include it in the culture of the home or hospital. Which songs does the person like at Christmas, what does he or she like to do? Christmas is about many things: eating and drinking, playing games and music, dancing, nativity. What is their favourite Christmas film? Can we bring the film to life? Shall we dance together to a Christmas song, waltz around the room singing 'I'm Dreaming of a White Christmas' (Berlin 1940). A little dance can go a long way, a little joy in touch and being together in a song can warm the heart for a long time.

Multi-sensory approaches to dance

A multi-sensory approach to dementia care is fun. Walking into a room where there is colour and texture, sound and scent is a creative, alive experience, making us feel awake and curious. Interactivity can be promoted through the arts, helping a person to stay connected to people and place. Fabrics which we can wear, draped over knees or shoulders, hats, scarves and flowers to put on or hold against our skin, all awaken and stimulate our presence. They help us to enjoy being here.

Many of us like to dress up. We enjoy wrapping ourselves up in fabrics and looking at ourselves in the mirror. Dressing up and make-up sessions can be lots of fun in care, and once a person is dressed up they may feel inclined to make a little dance! We may have associations with the costume the person has chosen and we may respond to them as the character they are creating. If someone reminds us of a princess we can respond to them as a princess; if someone is a king then we can behave towards them as if they are a king. They might be a belly dancer, they might be a fairy queen, they might be a fortune teller. We can make dances around them and with them, responding to the character they have become. We are in the land of the imagination, but we are touching a truth that rarely shows itself day to day.

Little dances

Our dances are like dandelion seeds, they grace the air with momentary movement. It is lovely to watch the movements people make, to enjoy these little dances day to day. Dances do not need to be grand or flamboyant; they can be simple gestures of self expression. We can look for the dances people are making quietly as they live their lives.

Sometimes we may feel that people with dementia are making automatic movements, which seem to have hold of them. We see repetitive actions of self soothing, of anxiety, of anger. It is worth sitting with these movements and wondering what is being communicated and what could be acknowledged and how. We do not want to dismiss the feelings in the movements and we do not want to abandon the person to the prison which repetitive movements can make. It is important to respond from our hearts and to allow our own bodies to communicate that we have heard the message and that we can participate in freeing the energy of the movement a little.

So first we stay with the movement, whether or not we feel it is expressive or stuck, and we try to feel it ourselves. Then we see if there is a way of allowing the movement more flow, which would allow the movement to transform itself into a slightly different movement that might offer some healing presence. These movements cannot be prescribed; they are born from empathy and love.

Moving with someone is an act of active listening. It is a willingness to accept their full being, their situation and their response to it. It is a belief that dancing can bring change. I have been very influenced by the wonderful dancing elder, Anna Halprin (1995), during my life. Anna believes that we are all part of an organic process and that movement keeps this connection alive. When someone moves very little we can still be there to notice the little movements of the body and to respond to them to make opportunity for them to grow and be expressed.

Emily makes shaking and flapping movements with her hands. I can respond by taking these shaking and flapping movements into my own body, letting them stream through my hands and fingers as if I am sending ripples through water. It is simply an imaginative way of responding to her. If I feel an intense energy coming through her movements, I can release it through the movements I make and find a quieter pool of energy after this expression, which can be shared. Working closely and empathically with someone means that I can express some of their story through my own body.

Dances with softness

Soft things bring us solace when we are disturbed. Soft things can express the energy of calm and love and gentleness. So we might bring in soft things to stimulate a dance. These soft things can be silky or velvety materials, which we can stroke or brush across our cheeks. Stroking movements with our hands are very soothing and can bring a feeling of tranquillity and joy. We can simply lay the piece of material across the person's lap and let them touch the material. We can pick up their movements and we can mirror them, making a little dance. We can enhance the experience of softness with music. Lullaby music is easy to find, either as instrumental or song. It weaves us into peacefulness together. This is a pleasant thing to do together at any point in the day. A little moment of beauty for everyone.

Dances with lightness

Balloons, bubbles and seaside windmills are all delightful things to bring into the dance. Passing round the windmills and blowing on them is good for the lungs and can bring memories of days by the seaside. Balloons and bubbles float on the air and might inspire us to reach up to touch them. Staff can put the balloons on a large cloth of stretchy lycra or silky material and gather round the edges to waft the balloons up high and then watch them descending. This is fun and makes a little community of imagination as we watch the balloons together. We can then take the movement of the balloons into our own bodies, wafting our arms up and down, forwards and then back into our laps.

Circle and partner dances

While we might find that it is only a few individuals who respond to the invitation to dance at first, it is still important to make dancing a community experience through the creation of the circle. In some dementia communities, people may still be physically able, still able to take each others' hands in a circle for a simple circle dance. Put on any music which suits the group, lively or slow and steady. The sequence of movements can be very simple, for example a few steps to the right and a few steps to the left, a few steps inwards, and few outwards. The steps are not as important as the sense of being a circle and making simple movements together to some music which is pleasurable. It might be one tune, it might be two, it might be more. If the dance is facilitated by someone who believes in its value it need not last a long time; the intention of connection will be received no matter the length of time. If there are enough staff, after the circle dance is done, people can move in partners and enjoy a little dance together in pairs. Again, no matter what ability, it is the intention of moving together, of enjoying the connection which is healing.

The dance of life

The movements that we make in our dancing sessions are all part of the dance of our lives. The movements that we express in accompaniment to music are moments from our being alive; they express our living presence. They are moments to be treasured. They are expressions of who we are and they affect the people we dance with. They ripple outwards. They connect us to each other. Dancing weaves us together.

5

Story: The Inner Text of our Lives

I enjoyed looking through a book of a resident's life which a psychologist had made. In it were photographs and important information about the person, her likes and dislikes. This book was for her and her carers to enjoy and to promote sensitivity towards the person. The book was not to be used as instruction or remedy, as a way of triggering memory or of trying to resurrect the ability to remember. The carer was not to ask questions about the photos because the inability to remember might create distress. The carer simply turned the pages with the person with dementia and watched for any response which they could meet with empathy.

We all have stories inside us. They are the inner text of our lives. We all have love and grief inside us. They are part of the emotional landscape of our lives. In dementia these stories are still floating inside us; they may need some expression. The arts are an opportunity for connection with our emotional landscape; they help us to enter into it and allow some of the stories to be told.

Stories can be told through pictures. If you gather a collection of images, which can be greeting cards and postcards, and spread them out on a table for someone to look at, they might linger on one particular picture, even pick it up, look at it more closely. It may be that something is speaking to them through the picture; it may be that the picture expresses something important in their life.

One woman chose an image of a snowy hillside walk, impulsively and intuitively knowing that it had some significance for her. As she looked at the picture she began to cry a little and to smile at the same time. For this image reminded her of the walks she used to take with her husband who was deceased. All the beauty and the sadness of their relationship was present in this image and it helped her to feel the value and the loss all at once. I do believe it is important to make time for the presence of loss in life. It is always a part of our stories.

In making a story about someone's life we celebrate the spirit of the person; we show that they matter, that they are important. Everyone's life is different and we can all learn from each other's lives and be inspired. There are many different ways of making stories, with different materials, in different relationships. As individuals we enjoy different methods of making. We can find out what the person prefers. We can use fabrics, paints, poetry, writing. The person may be able to make a substantial amount of their own story or they may need a lot of help in putting it together. Sometimes we need to make a story entirely for them through empathy, because the person is not capable.

An artistic presentation of someone's life is a deep acknowledgement of past life and present life. Stories made visible in some form in your dementia care setting are there for the person with dementia, for the relatives and for the staff to enjoy. These stories enter into us and affect us. They show us that we are all part of each other. They help us to empathize with each other. 'The moral genius of storytelling is that each, teller and listener, enters the space of the story for the other' (Frank 1995, p.18):

Writing reflection about a person shows how they have touched us and honours who they are. In the following reflection on my meeting with Millicent, I hope to highlight the gentle, loving kindness which emanated from her, bringing healing to me and others around her. Despite constantly losing track of what had happened that day, Millicent's heartful presence was powerful and strong. Over and over she wondered if there was a television in the room. Again and again she wondered if the doctors had been to see her that day, yet this did not seem to bother her greatly and for me it seemed unimportant in the presence of her beautiful self. She was kind and loving. 'Shall I talk to you, dear? Because I won't talk to you if you don't want me to.' 'How are you, dear?' 'We will miss our pal in the corner, won't we, dear?' I don't think we ever did get to answer the question of the television in the room, but we had some nice conversations about the programmes we liked to watch. Sometimes the concern is not the most important issue and it is the deeper contact that is being sought all the while.

Collage is always very popular in story-making because it is inclusive. People can participate in ways which are possible for them. They can indicate pictures they like in magazines, or they can cut them out and stick them down. It can be a restful community activity with everyone sitting round the table together, music playing, exchange of associations and memories. With a mix of staff and residents, people begin to find pictures which they feel belong to another's story, to cut them out and place them down by the other to see if they like them; to see if they want them in their story. These collages can be a moment in time, an array of images which are meaningful to the person at that moment. Or the collage can be more structured. It can be the life story of the person with moments from different periods of their life.

There might be songs which go with the images. It might be possible to perform the collage, taking an image into movement, making a little dance which conveys the feelings in the picture. We can move from one medium to another to embellish the story, to communicate it in different ways.

Making performances of people's lives makes them special and important; it gives them a place in the community. It is like having a birthday, being celebrated. Bringing a person's favourite songs and dances into the circle conveys a strong message of respect for the individual.

Making performances

Making performances about people's lives is dependent upon our connections with each other. We cannot make a performance about someone's life from a place of detachment. We need to feel close to the person; we need to imagine ourselves in the shoes of that person. Knowing that our physical and psychological security is so dependent upon our sensed connection with others, the sensitive depiction of someone's life can become a deep root of security for a person with dementia. Here is how we have made performances of people's lives.

BEING WITH THE PERSON

The first step in making a performance about someone is to be with them, to feel their presence. As Sarah has written in Chapter 3, sometimes people want company and sometimes not. If we are allowed into the space of relationship with the person we can begin to connect with them and to appreciate their being. There is a person behind the dementia who is present and who needs to be noticed.

RESEARCHING A LIFE

The person's story may be told with song. In Chapter 3, Sarah has shown how she asks the person which songs they like. She researches the songs so that she knows them by heart and can sing them. We do not need to have accompaniment. We can sing the songs from our hearts, one person to another. There does not need to be a verbal response to the song for us to know that it has touched the person. Sometimes people hum along softly, sometimes they join in with the words, sometimes they smile, sometimes they cry.

The person's story may be told with objects. We can find out what the person loves; it might be the beach, the woods, the mountains. It might be sewing, dancing, fishing, engines, coins. Once we have found out we can research that thing which aroused the interest and passion of the person in the past. We can then bring in objects to touch and hold. These objects might be comforting or they might awaken sadness. We have to be prepared for many emotions. We have to be prepared to be surprised; to allow the responses. The value of this research is that it enables us to find ways of reaching the person inside, of perceiving the story of a life.

The person's story may be told with pictures. We can find photographs and paintings which we feel represent some of the things we know about the person. We can research art with ease on the internet, typing in themes or names that we know to see what we can find. We can bring these photographs and images to the person and wait to see if there is any response.

If the person with dementia likes to use arts materials, we can gather together a selection of different media. Air-drying clay is great because it is soft and malleable for hands which may not be strong. Paints, pastels and chalks are also very accessible. Fabrics, buttons and stones can be felt and placed together in different formations. Staff members can facilitate the process of making by being attentive, by asking where the person would like to place the craft materials.

There is also the possibility of making a soft toy or puppet which symbolizes things that are of importance to the person. We can show the person all kinds of fabrics and find out who and what brings them comfort now. We can ask the person to choose favourite colours and textures, a favourite animal, a favourite person. Then we can begin to make a soft toy or puppet with the fabric and craft materials at our disposal. Buttons, wooden spoons, garden sticks, pipe-cleaners, rubber bands, staplers, cotton wool, are all useful bits and pieces for making.

KEEPING COMPANY IN MAKING

When we are working towards making a story of someone's life, the process of making is important. It does not matter how adept we are, what matters is the connection between us. Sitting with someone, quietly making is a healing experience. Sometimes we talk and sometimes not. Sometimes the person with dementia joins in and sometimes not. When we are being creative time slows down, we feel peaceful and we make time for the other to be. We exchange presence. We are contentedly immersed in our activity in the present moment. We can use whatever craft skills we have: it may be knitting, crocheting, quilting, to make something which represents the person's life.

LISTENING AND RESPONDING

In listening for someone's life we need to be open to how they are. When we discover music, pictures or movements which they like, we can experience the music, the picture and the movements for ourselves and notice how we are affected by them. These are artistic ways in to feeling what it might be like to be that person. Once we have some elements to use in the story we can begin to be creative. We can put together a series of of music, song, picture, craftwork, dance and movement to make a performance for the person. We can show it to the person and, if they wish, to the circle of people in the dementia care setting. It is important that everyone has a turn who wants one. Even if there is no ending performance, the process of gathering together a life is still significant and valuable.

Animals

Animals are a source of comfort in the lives of many people. Cats and dogs often play a big part in the story of someone's life. It is helpful if animals are present in the dementia care setting, so that people can stroke them and be with them. Animals communicate in silent ways. Their presence can be healing.

When making collage people often choose images of animals. Sometimes they are special memories of pets, sometimes it is as if the presence of the animal has something to offer. The strength of the elephant, the power of the horse, the affection of the dog, the softness of the rabbit in some way reaches us and gives us something. Animal calendars contain beautiful images to look at together. They can be cut out and stuck down as part of the collage.

Stories and the family

It is good to invite involvement from the family in the creation of the story. Stories are about valuing a person's life past and present. They help us to gain a vision of the person's life and to celebrate the spirit of the person. We can ask all members of the family and friendship groups to supply pictures and thoughts about the person in this co-creative work. Often families feel not only regret but guilt for leaving a parent in a residential or nursing care home. Creative involvement in the making of the story is a way of coming to terms with these complex feelings. Creativity is often a multi-layered process in which feelings surface, evolve and come to rest in a more peaceful place. In thinking deeply about the parent, about all the parent has done for us and meant to us in our lives, we make contact with the relational bond which binds us together, and we may feel that we make contact with the inner life of that person. Making a picture about our parent, writing a poem about our parent, thinking of a song which he or she loves brings us close to the parent in a different way than in day-to-day contact. It magnifies the existence of the other and gives us a perspective on our relationship. It helps us to let go of the past and move into the present.

Being present with a person with dementia can feel like being present with the loss of them. It is a strange and numbing paradox. Yet this numbing feeling is anchored in a resistance to let them be how they are now, and a resistance to the pain and grief we feel. Writing stories about our grief can help us to move through the grief into a place of acceptance and tranquillity. All our pools of tears are little oases on the journey towards peacefulness in the present moment.

Story and the present moment

Finally, what we need to accept is that the stories we make in the present moment are little fragments of being to be enjoyed and appreciated now. In dementia the sense of a linear life has gone. We cannot reclaim it for the person with dementia, but we can enjoy the panorama of their life ourselves, as it is comforting to us and gives us a sense of the purpose and meaning in all of our lives. In dementia though, it is perhaps more important to realize that the fragments of a life floating randomly in the mind are fulfilling another purpose than chronological coherence. There is perhaps a different coherence at play. I could call this an emotional coherence. I feel that the emotional memories lying in the body and mind make a storyline in themselves, a story of the heart, a story which is still being played out during our dementia.

Memories and present feelings coalesce in a song, a movement, a picture. Feelings reawaken and pour out. This process is the organic flow of feelings inside us which has its own rhythm and its own purpose. The flow of feelings is not at the command of the rational brain; it has its own impulse, its own stream. If we can enter into this world and time of feeling with another we offer them the opportunity to be in the stream of life they find themselves in. Some of the stories may not make much sense to us, but they do have an expressive impulse and therefore a need to emerge. We can receive them however random they may feel. We can trust that they are part of an expressive design.

If we can accept the feelings and at the same time not be overwhelmed by them, then they will pass. We need to try not to block the feelings and yet at the same time gain a perspective on them. If we feel that the anger being expressed is not the person but the disease, we can learn to hold the anger safely and to let it go. We can imagine ourselves catching it briefly and then letting it down into a stream to float away down river. Other times we may feel that the feelings are coming from a deeper place, from the person's heart and that they are being freed from a locked cellar of the past. These feelings need a safe haven too and we can receive them for the person again before laying them down to rest.

Symbolism

Often when we think of someone, we are affected by their presence. We might imagine them as an element of nature, as water, as fire, as air, as earth; we might imagine them as a rock, a stone, a flower, a tree. We might have associations and memories about them, particular songs which seem to represent them, or paintings, or objects. It is good to notice these intuitive connections because they bring us closer to the essence of the person with dementia. Such connections can be the starting point of a symbolic consciousness of the person, and the beginnings of a story.

Often the person has an object that they need to have near them, or particular places they like to sit, things they like to touch or hold. These things are often not simply of physical significance. They hold an emotional and psychological power as well. We know that people with dementia thrive better in familiar surroundings with things around them that they know. When we surround ourselves with these things we are enfolding ourselves in our stories, the special moments and the special people in our lives.

In choosing the encircling environment with this symbolic consciousness for the person with dementia, we participate in story-making. We carefully create a storied home which can reach the person silently and slowly. Sometimes it is not the old familiar things a person wants; we need to spend time with them now to find out what stimulates a response, what awakens and what comforts them now.

6

Group Case Studies: People with Dementia and their Families

In this chapter I look at how the creative arts have been helpful in working with groups of people with dementia, their families and friends. The families and friends of people with dementia are frequently forgotten; the feelings of loss, regret, guilt, desperation, sorrow and anger have no dedicated space to be heard and acknowledged. It is difficult to learn how to be with someone who has changed so much. Coming to terms with our real feelings about this change is a step towards being able to be with them in the present moment.

The creative arts can provide a means of expressing, releasing and coming to terms with such difficult feelings. One such example in the previous chapter is working with story to invite expression, letting go and coming into the present with the loved one with dementia. The arts can provide an opportunity to build a new relationship with the person with dementia. They can also help to forge strong empathic contact between the staff and the patient or client in all dementia care settings.

To illustrate how family processes can be facilitated, here is a story by Carly Marchant, registered movement psychotherapist, which shows how music and movement can be used to rebuild broken bridges between people with dementia and their families and friends.

Being with: finding an approach to joining the individual who has dementia in the present space and time
Carly Marchant

This story is a personal account of how I find a sensitive way of being with people with dementia and their families. In this story I share my experiences, insights and strategies in working in the present time and space. I am trying to give the people whom I work with acceptance and to reinstate purpose and dignity.

The assumption is sometimes made that dementia is like a second childhood, but as the Royal College of Psychiatrists propose (2009), it is not. A child is a developing person; an individual presenting with dementia is a deteriorating being. Not only have they lost touch with the person they used to be: the amorous spouse, the caring parent and the diligent home maker or professional, but they are losing the connection with their families and friends. These loved ones have lost sight of their own role and may wonder how they can ever be with their beloved one again.

When I first tried to understand the term dementia, I was overwhelmed by the description: absence of thought, losing sight of myself, disconnecting from my body and my environment. Dementia feels such a daunting prospect: like slowly entering into a dark, lonely world of no return. Time filters away like sand in an egg timer turned upside down, as I return inevitably back to earth, gradually losing consciousness. I am swallowed up by time into timelessness, present in body but sifting away in mind.

I cannot contemplate what this would truly feel like and I feel overshadowed by the pain and grief this must bring to the individual with dementia and their loved ones. I can identify with families of people with dementia as some years ago a close family member of mine received the devastating news that they had this cruel disease. At first this news was difficult for me to accept, especially as my relative was so young. My first thought was 'how this can happen?' He was only in his late fifties. I soon discovered that early onset was extremely common, currently affecting more than 15,000 people under the age of 65 in the UK (Alzheimer's Society 2007). My emotions were in turmoil, protesting against the injustice, then I felt guilty that my emotions were overwhelming me. How must my relative be feeling in the knowledge of the fate that was mapped out for the rest of his life? How can you accept that your body and mind are slowly disintegrating before your eyes, while your eyes will not recognize this deterioration? It was a cruel fact that my relative would lose sight of himself, but I and the rest of my family would not.

This horror was deeply ingrained in my mind and body when beginning my first placement during my training as a dance movement psychotherapist. I was to facilitate a dance movement psychotherapy group with families of people with dementia. I decided that I wanted to use my own personal experience and understanding to inform and help others who were going through this devastating experience. I felt extremely anxious about confronting my fears while in the professional role as therapist, but felt it was right to stay close to my feelings and experiences as they could bring me closer to others who had received similar devastating news. Having been touched by dementia myself, I felt driven to find a way of being with people with dementia in the present and to find a way for others in a similar position to me.

The individual with dementia may have lost their ability to remember, take care of themselves, fulfil their role as a family and society member, but it does not mean that they cannot ever be with themselves and their family again. The family can find a new way of being with them, accepting and tuning into their world in the present space and time. This is where I would like you, the reader, to come on a journey of rediscovery with me, to accompany me on my quest to learn how to be with the individual who has dementia. I will write to you about my experiences as a then trainee therapist, offering a case study from my heartfelt experience, which has given me much encouragement in my role as both therapist and family member. It has helped me to gain an understanding and acceptance of this shattering disease.

The setting of my story is a 30-bed inpatient ward for people with dementia in a secure mental health hospital. The patients range between 50 and 80 years of age and are of mixed gender and cultural backgrounds. They share the commonality of their diagnosis of dementia and that they are unsafe to live independently in the community, presenting either a risk of harm to themselves or others. The patients are split between two wards, one assigned to female patients and the other male. Distributed between the two wards is a multidisciplinary team who offer support and knowledge to maintain and encourage the individual's independence. The multidisciplinary team comprises a wide range of professionals, including consultant psychiatrists, registered mental health nurses, occupational therapists, social workers and mental health support workers. There are no arts therapists at this setting and it is the team's first experience of having a trainee arts therapist work alongside them on a placement.

Prior to the establishment of the dance movement psychotherapy group, I conducted assessments including risk and appropriateness for group work. I spent a couple of weeks visiting the wards to make observations before commencing the sessions. This is a sample of some of my main perceptions of the patients, setting and environment, and family and friends visiting hour.

The patients' bodies
- absence of thought and expression

- haunted expressions

- lifelessness suggested by long periods of empty stillness
- thin, fragile bodies, decaying teeth
- gargling vocal sounds, shouting, verbal abuse directed towards other patients or staff
- Slack jaw, loose open mouth
- tired or sleeping bodies slumped on chairs lined up in a row. In one instance an individual slumped on the floor
- sudden, repetitive, fidgety movements (particularly with hands)
- shuffling through the space with hunched postures.

The setting
- institutionalized decoration, pastel and flowery patterns throughout
- pungent smell of urine
- chairs lined up in a row on both sides of the room
- an empty dining table
- wheelchairs and frames scattered around the room
- doors securely locked and a doorbell occasionally ringing to indicate family, friends or staff arriving
- staff members hurrying round the space
- an observatory staff room overlooking the lounge area
- some individuals confined to their beds in small rooms containing single beds, a wardrobe and a bedside unit.

Family and friends visiting hour
- sadness
- grief-stricken individuals trying to communicate with their loved one
- holding and stroking their loved one's hand
- witnessing verbal or physical abuse towards themselves or others
- hearing a range of different emotions
- witnessing the isolation of the loved one
- witnessing the loved one asleep
- terrified expressions
- minimal verbal communication
- sitting on a chair next to their loved one, gazing at their absent face.

These are only a handful of perceptions, but they represent well the general mood and emotions present among the people on this ward or visiting the ward. Recording my perceptions helped me to realize how much the individuals with the disease were suffering, and how much distress their family and friends were experiencing. Visitors clearly displayed sadness, loss, grief, despair and terror. Witnessing these sad meetings inspired me to create joint sessions for patients, families and friends. After discussing this with the multidisciplinary team, I was permitted to offer a session for families and friends to find a new way to be with their loved ones. The next step was for me to explain my work to the patients and to their families and friends and to give them an invitation to participate. Invitations were willingly accepted by three pairs, so now it was time to pilot my ideas.

It was a sunny Thursday morning and I arrived at the hospital ready to take my first-ever joint dance movement psychotherapy session with patients and their families and friends. I felt nervous. The idea sounded simple: invite the family members and friends to join the patient where they are. But I felt the pressure to make it happen and I did not know how, which was anxiety-provoking. I remember thinking that I needed to trust the process and that perhaps my insecurity would give me an insight into the life of the individual suffering from the disease. I felt like I was taking a huge risk walking in without any solutions or methods; but I knew in my heart that what mattered was that I was fully present and self-aware. If I could embody these qualities then I was communicating something to others about a way to be with the patients.

I entered the ward and checked in with the relevant staff team. It was confirmed that three patients and three family members or friends would be attending. As I walked on to the ward I became aware of the usual reactions that greeted my arrival. I began to set up the lounge room that had been allocated for the session and found a safe space in the room to store my props consisting of different shapes and sizes of fabric, a stretch band known as a 'co-oper band' and a case full of various music. I formed a circle of chairs and greeted the people as they filtered through into the space. Two of the patients were able to walk slowly into the space assisted by their family member or friend, and one patient was pushed in a wheelchair. I invited the group to sit in this circle as a way of coming together.

After the initial introduction and greeting, I invited the group to move to some music from the soundtrack of the film *Amelie* (Jeunet 2001), a track called 'Guilty' (Whiting, Akst and Kahn 1931). The group soon became aware that they were moving in unison with a shared rhythm, while being encouraged to follow the needs of their own bodies. The music was gentle and was from an Edwardian era waltz in 4/4 timing. This music facilitated dancing together. Immediately their eyes lit up and they were able to find a way of joining with each another in movement, no matter how minimal. This created a vehicle for them to be, and to belong together, without judgement.

The patients and family member or friend felt joy. They could laugh once again, joke at how they were moving in or out of time. Somehow the dancing did not require anyone to fulfil a role; it just allowed the deep intuitive core of the person to be present. In the dance both partners could sense a place of belonging together, beyond the definitions and expectations of role.

After this piece of music, I played another, gentler piece of music, called 'Lovelorn' from the album *For Amelie* (Krull *et al.* 2004). The participants listened enthusiastically to the lyrics, which captured the feelings of loss and abandonment that most of us feel when our loved ones seem distant, retreating from us, gone. There is an image given of water trickling through sand, the past seeping away with memories of soulful connection. They responded with tears of joy and sadness, uncontrollable laughter and revitalized bodies. Several of them joined in, singing the words or softly humming.

The lyrics of the song helped the participants to tune into their own feelings of loss and sadness, of desire to reconnect. As I witnessed the pairs coming together in movement I felt happy. The participants had been able to see themselves again, to love again, laugh again, join again in the present. No matter how severe the grip of the disease, the dance had let partners be together intuitively, even if only for a short time.

They say that dementia robs you of your faculties and therefore of your dignity. Yet in this dancing together, dignity arose from the essential contact between people. The movement experience in response to the lyrics of the song reminds us of what is missing and what can be found again.

Intense and 'difficult' emotions

Most of us feel strong and overwhelming emotions when a parent, grandparent or close relative changes with dementia. We may feel frustrated and angry because of the loss of connection and communication. We may feel guilty and worthless because we feel we are not doing the best thing for our loved one in choosing residential care for them. But we do not feel equipped to care for them at home. Nor does the government encourage home care for those with dementia with appropriate funding as in foster care; so we may feel depressed and helpless. We may also feel lonely, tired and unloved ourselves. Such feelings are very common, but we do not talk about them. Why not, if they are so common? It feels good to find out that there are so many of us with these feelings and to have the opportunity to share them. 'A burden shared is a burden halved', as the saying goes.

When our loved one loses their language and they do not remember us, when they act irrationally and seem not be themselves any longer, we may feel lost and bewildered. We may feel an overwhelming wish that this was not happening and that we could 'fix' things, make things 'right' again. Our loved one may become very controlling and it may be that we respond by being very controlling too. But this response may not be the most helpful one.

When swamped by overwhelming feelings a common response is to resist them; they are too painful. But with time it may be possible, though, to let ourselves feel them and begin to let go of them. The answer to pain is not control of self or others, or clinging to the past. We remain stuck if we do this, unable to move forward in our lives. If we can let go and give in to the present moment, the present situation, allowing ourselves to have our feelings, then we can make contact with something which lies beyond the functioning of the brain; we make contact with the deeper life of the heart.

In the 2005 documentary made by Tony Robinson, *Me and My Mum* (Robinson 2005), there is a reference to care based on love and listening. Once we dip down beneath the language and beneath the desire to control, fix and change, we can find a deeper place of connection through love. Tony Robinson noticed how from a state of agitation, manifested in body tension and growling sounds, his mum would stop and smile at him when he arrived at the home 'because she loves me'.

The creative arts and letting go

Life is full of hidden surprises. None of us knows what is in store. Life jolts us sometimes and presents us with things which are shocking and difficult to contemplate. The creative arts can help to ease our minds into our present circumstances because they are gentle, metaphoric and indirect. Jung (1979) writes this about the creative process:

> The creative process has a feminine quality, and creative work arises from unconscious depths... Whenever the creative force predominates, life is ruled and shaped by the unconscious rather than by the conscious will, and the ego is swept along on an underground current, becoming nothing more than a helpless observer of events. (Jung 1979, p.103)

By letting go into a creative process we let something else take over. This something else is an organic process, which helps us to come to terms with things as they are now. It helps us to be in the present with ourselves and others. Recently my life was under threat and I have used the creative arts to show me a way to be so that I am in touch with my reality and in touch with my needs. I let the art do the talking and it shows me the way forwards.

There are many different media available in the creative arts. Some of us may move with freedom or sing or paint or use clay with freedom. It is important to find an art medium which you feel comfortable with, which you feel at home with; something which flows with your being. This flow may not at first seem easy to find, but with daily practice it is possible. The first thing to do is to make your link with the medium. We all have media which call us for some reason; they attract us, they demand our attention. Stay with this first impulse towards the medium and begin your friendship with it through practice. You can buy yourself a pad and pastels or paints, some clay, a writing book, some beautiful pens, some music, or make space for movement. Prepare the ground. Then make time to spend in creative process. Let your mind hover towards your present circumstances and relationships and your feelings about these. Then let your body move or your hands make, or let your voice sing and hum. Let yourself be swept up in a creative process like Jung describes above. You will probably find that feelings surface powerfully and sweep you on in your creativity, helping you to let go of the old feelings and making space for the new.

When someone changes or leaves us they take a little piece of us with them. We are not the same anymore, just as they are not the same. The loss of them is also a loss in us; it can feel like the loss of a shared past. This parting is often painful and we need to help ourselves through our discomfort. The arts can help us to do this, because they make a space for the true feelings of loss and grief to flow outwards. This outward flow is important because it means that we stay in the tide of life, forever moving forwards tumbling into life as it is in the present moment.

Death

Sarah remembers a time of parting in a home where she works. Here, singing together provided a necessary shared ritual of ending, a completion and a celebration of happy times together.

In another home, I was invited to sing with a group of friends who had collected around the bed of a lady, Jeanette, who was dying. When I went in, her husband and friends were chatting and nattering as I imagined they had often done before. Jeanette was lying in bed, eyes closed, her breathing shallow, and yet the conversation around her seemed natural, easy, a mixture of the day's news, and reminiscences. There was no sense of stress, or the tension of unexpressed grief. The friends were clear on what song to sing, 'I Love a Lassie' (Lauder and Grafton 1905), as they had enjoyed singing old-style songs together so often. So we all sang, smiling, swaying and looking at one another, and Jeanette. The friends were sharing this moment together, sharing Jeanette's last moments together. I was struck by the easiness among these friends at the time of death. I imagined they had been friends for years, been out as couples together, shared many experiences, and now, here was the next experience to share. How wonderful for Jeanette's husband to have such loving support as his wife died. They were lifelong friends for sure.

But what did singing the song do? I believe it brought the friends even closer together. They had clearly sung this song before, probably on many occasions. Perhaps they were remembering good times; times they had shared laughing, dancing, eating and drinking, remembering, and further consolidating their friendship. And for Jeanette? Comfort perhaps in the sound of familiar voices, being together as they had done before, being with her in friendship, through her last moments of her life, and into her death. I see that as courageous. When people I know well have died, I have found myself feeling physical responses to my grief: sickness, pallor, aching in my very bones and cells. Wanting to run away from grief and busying myself in everyday tasks so there's no gap for the sadness to sneak through, yet it always does. It is far healthier to express our full emotional response to death at the time it happens than to hold on to, and cover up this natural response, only for that to make us unwell, and affect our lives later on.

7

Group Case Studies: People with Dementia and their Staff

In this chapter I reflect upon the findings of the Skills for Care dementia project in which both Sarah and I were involved. It makes a good forum for discussion of the benefits of the creative arts in dementia care and, in particular in this chapter, for discussion of the benefits to staff in the work which they do. As we shall find, the attention to staff wellbeing, provided through creative arts work, constitutes a rich investment in the service for people with dementia in a number of ways. The benefits may be summarized as empathy with self, empathy with other staff and empathy with service users.

Context

A developmental project seeking to explore the enhancement of care for people with dementia was commissioned by the Skills for Care Involvement Team during the period 2008–09 in East and West Sussex. The research question for the project was: 'How can therapeutic relationships and environments that safeguard and enhance the wellbeing of older people with dementia be developed in social care services?' The two aspects of potential enhancement explored by the project were (i) dementia care mapping (originated and developed by the Bradford Dementia Group at Bradford University) and (ii) the creative arts. This chapter will describe and evaluate the creative arts component of the project.

Three creative arts professionals: Anne Colvin, independent dance artist and choreographer, Jill Hayes (myself), dance movement psychotherapist and Sarah Povey, voice movement therapist, were employed to conduct and evaluate the contribution of the creative arts to in-service training for staff in residential and nursing care settings. Specifically, we were responsible for the development and delivery of seven two-day training courses. A total of 67 staff attended these training courses.

The project was underpinned by the concept of person-centred care, which is the core principle of both dementia care mapping and creative arts practice (Innes and Hatfield 2004)

> The core functions of the healing arts therapies in the care of persons with dementia are the reclamation, the regeneration and the celebration of the human spirit. These are also the primary goals of person-centered care. Each of these therapies flows from a similar deep concern for the support of personhood and the wellbeing of the individual. Each has a concern for the fullness of life, and puts connection, interaction and communication, both verbal and non-verbal, at the top of the list of priorities in terms of care goals. The healing arts therapies and person-centered care are natural partners. (Innes and Hatfield 2004, p.9)

A significant finding of the project was that care staff found the use of creative and reflective approaches especially helpful in developing self-empathy and empathy with others. It enabled staff to change task-centred practice to person-centred practice by the use of activities such as singing, dance and drama.

What did we do?

A key aim throughout the training was reflective practice through the creative arts. Each creative session was designed with this in mind. We focused on relaxation and playing together, the expressive use of movement, sometimes with props and music, the value of touch, reminiscence with pictures, photographs and objects, drama, singing, collage, drawing and using colour. The key objectives in all of the creative processes were: self-listening and listening to others, expression, catharsis and change. The feedback from participants on their own learning from the creative activities centred upon:

1. compassion and empathy

2. communication and trust

3. feelings in professionalism

4. patience

5. spontaneity.

The activities introduced to staff enabled them to immerse themselves in creative activity, engaging with an inner experience. When we immerse in this way, we are not simply taking part and walking away unchanged. We are letting ourselves drop into our emotions and we are internally affected by this. We are meeting both ourselves and others on different ground, ground which is not so dependent upon external identity, ground where we meet as equals, in the flux and flow of feeling.

The activities

The activities were usually conducted in the complete staff group, including managers. Sometimes we used whole group activities, sometimes activities in pairs or small groups. The rationale behind training together was that in awakening our empathy through creativity in interaction with each other, we will be able to bring such creative empathy into our work with people with dementia. The following are some of the activities we used on the training.

Pictures of you

For this activity you need a wide selection of images. They can be cards and postcards which you have collected over time. Invite the people in the group to let themselves be drawn towards an image without knowing why. Then invite each person to find a partner in the same way, drawn towards each other intuitively.

Then encourage each partner to freefall their associations and memories triggered by the image, while the other partner listens holding the Chinese character for 'to listen' (see Chapter 3) in their hearts. When one partner has finished, the other can respond in different ways. One way is simply to recall all that they felt while listening. Another is to respond in movement, again recalling the 'kairos' moments (the moments when the person was fully present emotionally) (see Chapter 2) from the partner's story. The end result of this activity is often profound and brings people together in empathy. Words have not obscured the visual and felt emotions surfacing in the activity. The emotions have been received and accepted. Most participants feel deeply listened to and seen. This alters the relationship they have with their work colleague. The colleague becomes a trusted person, someone who has insight into their life and understanding of who they are. It is possible to work more easily with this person now, because of this mutual understanding.

Symbolic objects

Another variation on this theme is to invite staff to bring in objects which represent themselves or perhaps which represent how they perceive each other or their service users. If the focus is on self, we can explore the aspects of the object which we identify with. If the focus is on others, we can explore our perceptions of the other person through the symbolic associations we make. This kind of creative sharing releases us into new ways of connecting with each other because images and symbols do not tie us in knots of explanation. They open us up to the internal world of feeling, imagination and memory, which is present whenever we come into contact with each other, but we usually choose to ignore it. The exploration of our perceptions, whether of self or the other, reveals much about our internal world. We share ourselves both when we reflect upon an object to represent self and when we reflect upon the object we have chosen to represent another. Symbolic reflection such as this brings people closer together; it enhances empathy.

Memory baskets

Bring in a big basket or sack filled with unusual objects collected from charity shops, jumble sales or car boot sales. Ask the group to close their eyes. Pass the basket round and invite the participants to feel for an object. Ask them to feel its shape and texture. Ask them to imagine whom it belonged to. Ask them to imagine what colour it is. Ask them to make up a story in their minds about the object. Then invite them to open their eyes and to look at the object in their hands.

Then, in pairs, ask each partner to listen to the other as the story of their encounter with the object is told. Encourage the listener to give their response to this story and to relay the moments when the partner becomes energized, alive. Again, in such sharing, we are witnessing our colleague in a new way, a person whose imagination, memories and feelings are of value. This different way of perceiving our colleagues becomes mirrored in the way we perceive our service users.

Sharing movements

In a circle, so that everyone can see everyone else, we put on some music which the group has chosen and we warm up together, using all the body parts in turn, then moving with the whole body. Sometimes lots of different styles of music and movement are present, being chosen by different members of the group. This creates a chance for people to teach each other different movements and dance styles. We share with each other something of our family and our culture when we do this. Through our bodies we show what is important in our hearts.

Sometimes the movements become more idiosyncratic, more expressive of the individual inside. When someone makes a movement, encourage the whole group to try the movement on and feel what it feels like from the inside. How do they feel when they indulge in this movement? How would they like to change it to make it their own? By sharing ourselves in movement in this way we create fluidity for ourselves; we are expressing our inner life, reaching out to others; letting them respond to us from their own felt sense. This can be a meaningful exchange, yet light and free. We understand each other differently though embodiment.

Dressing up

To develop the previous activity, it is possible to dress up in beautiful fabrics, wrapping them around our bodies however we wish. We can bring in hats and scarves, along with large pieces of fabric made of different materials, cotton, silk, satin, linen, lycra and so on. Flowing silks are lovely for expression of feeling and lycra is good for contact between people, pulling and stretching, wafting or wrapping.

Once people are dressed up they can begin to play using movement and song. We might find that the costumes freely created suggest a scene, a song or a type of dance in which the group can become involved. There may be several stories wanting to be told and we can accommodate them all, with appreciation for the diversity in the room. Using each person in turn we can begin to create a little dance or scene around them to embellish their costume or character. This is fun and can make the person feel appreciated and listened to.

Making pictures of our experience

When the more vigorous activities involving movement have subsided, it is often useful to make a picture in order to process the experience. Lay out large and small sheets of paper with pastels or paints and invite the group to record on the page their experience of moving and dancing. This is a gentle reflective time and you can keep the music playing according to the group's request. Sometimes it feels right to work in silence. Ask the group what it wants.

Encourage the group to freefall their experience onto the page, noticing if they are judging their picture, and in the noticing letting the judgement go. It is as if they can keep on dancing on the page, letting colours and shapes be chosen spontaneously. The picture does not have to be anything prescribed. It does not have to be a literal representation of events. It is an impression and an expression of the feeling and quality of the experience, which can be shared with another group member or in the group circle, or both. The picture becomes a vehicle for sharing the inner experience, and for knowing one's own internal experience and the internal experience of someone else.

This is your life

Invite the group to make a collage of their life. This can be done however they like. One way is to imagine yourself back in time as you once were at a certain age. There might be a particular time of childhood, adolescence or young and mature adulthood which is strong in your memory. You are still very aware of the feelings of that time, of the joys, the losses, the hope, the sadness. You can let your feelings emerge and help you to choose the image from the magazine or calendar to represent that time in your life. You can let your feelings help you to create the panorama of your life to be shared with another.

The staff who took part in this activity felt deeply moved and inspired. Recalling and recording imaginatively the peak moments from your life gives meaning to it. It gives respect and dignity to your life. There is also a sense of purpose. This is what my life is about; this is what is important to me. There may be a sense of development and change over time, but in each moment of my life there was something which drove me, something which gave me a meaning, and which led into the next phase. This meaning may be connected to divine faith or human faith; there is no prescription for purpose. What is vital is that each person finds something which moves and inspires *them*, something which is true for *them*. Even when life has been lived in periods of depression and difficulty, there are moments when the tide turns and hope appears again.

The arts provide an imaginative way of discovering and communicating passions and values which arise from the individual's experience of life.

In creating their personal life stories staff enjoyed expressing the thread of purpose which joined the parts of their life together. Engaging with this activity can have a profound effect upon our perspective of the lives of others. The person with dementia has, like us, lived most of their lives as an independent adult with projects and intentions. We need to remember this when we are with them. It alters how we see them. It bestows respect.

More difficult for us still in the mainstream of intentional life, is to value the phase the person with dementia finds themselves in now. Intentions are fast flowing away; the person moves round and round in little eddies, having drifted into a hollow in the bank of the river. This could be a time of quiet, all intentions gone away; simply a time to enjoy the pool, the water, the colours, the light. Our main concern is that we have a peaceful time as we move towards death. Perhaps this is the purpose of the last stage of life (as in the epigraph poem by Cathy French at the beginning of the book).

To see how Sarah applies some of the singing activities conducted in the dementia project to her workplace in a specific residential and nursing care setting, we introduce you to the 'Lively sessions' involving trainers, staff and residents altogether. From these examples we shall see clearly how the creative arts develop empathy between staff and residents.

Lively sessions

At one home a member of staff asked to be more involved in the sessions. She wanted to have the opportunity to sit and sing with the residents, as the staff used to, before their workload had increased. This inspired me to consider developing a session that both the residents and staff would enjoy. I wanted this session to not only enhance the relationship between staff and residents, but also to have the effect of adding to the residents' quality of life and improving the working environment for the staff. I decided to give the staff a little introductory session, just two hours, to creative arts therapies. I thought the best way for the staff to learn was to experience what I was intending to bring to the combined sessions. I covered the importance of becoming centred in ourselves, being in touch with our body and our emotions in the present moment. Learning to let go of other worries and concerns of our lives and being here, right now, with what was going on. We practised allowing our hearts to expand, feeling our love for ourselves, for nature, for the world and then looking at one another. This look was not a glance, not a fleeting moment, but really looking into one another's eyes, and becoming aware of how we feel with different people.

Working in pairs, we looked at our partner, remembering that we all have different experiences in our lives. We all have wondrous stories, delightful and tragic, and also worries and concerns. In short, we are basically the same, striving for happiness, and dealing with the experiences of our lives as best we can. We practised feeling love in our hands, and resting our hands on one another's shoulders and back, learning to understand the experience of this focused and purposeful touch. By becoming centred in ourselves we can relate with more compassion to those around us. Our centre is a place of authenticity.

Next we began to play, moving as we listened to various pieces of music in whatever way occurred to us, without care for how we looked, but with care for how we were feeling. We tried different ways of dancing: dancing with abandon, dancing in a way we perceived 'ugly'. This helped us to release self-consciousness, get us more connected to our bodies, and change our belief that we need to 'look good' when we move. Such joy and fulfilment can come from dancing with abandon. This goes for singing too, and in the session we sang together not focusing on whether we were in tune or not, but focusing on the enjoyment. Joan Baez talks about singing as being an act of love. The singer can reach directly into someone's heart, setting up a resonance of emotion. With this connection made, the two journey together, both affirmed by their shared experience. We played with our voices, singing as though we were at a rugby match, singing like punk rockers, singing in posh voices and whatever other characters and styles we could think of.

I recently heard an older gentleman recalling his music teacher at school. He said the best thing about music lessons was that, when they were singing, his teacher said to them that it didn't matter what they sounded like, it was important to enjoy yourself and sing with gusto. This is it exactly! Singing is innate in each one of us and so is dance and movement, if only we can get over our idea of having to do things right or look or sound 'pretty'. I would rather dance and sing with the real you than with some pretence of who you think you should be.

It saddens me that through the over-disciplining of learning to sing and to dance, spontaneity and innate expression are often lost. Singing or dancing is something that many of us go somewhere 'to do,' to be taught in a certain way, and if we feel we don't meet the 'standard' we may give it up completely. Yet we can sing and dance in every moment of every day; humming to ourselves as we shop, washing up with rhythmic flow, breathing the movement of the water as we walk by a river. Singing used to be integral in our communities. Miners used to sing on the way home from the mine; farm workers would get together and sing songs of harvesting, tilling, and sowing at the end of a day's hard graft; families would come together around a piano or squeeze box singing songs that passed down through generations. Singing and dancing could be integral in the daily lives of our communities and this is still the case in some cultures. Some societies in Africa seem to have a song for every event and every occasion, and these are not just saved for the big ones like weddings or birthdays. Following the floods in 2000 in Mozambique there was a news report that a village that had lost all its cattle was getting a new herd. The folk of the village gathered on the river bank where the animals were arriving. They sang as the animals arrived, and continued singing as they walked to the new pasture. It seemed that everyone was there: men, women, children and animals. This was a momentous occasion. The people were celebrating new life, a new start as well as welcoming the new herd. These people were so connected with nature and the present moment, so unified in their community. Why aren't we?

I sing many traditional folk songs as part of my work and many older people know these because they learnt them at school along with other songs they heard on the radio. Leaving aside the music teachers that stopped people singing, it is fantastic that traditional folk songs were being passed on in this way. I am not aware whether children are still learning such songs. I dearly hope so, though I doubt it. Let's start singing for joy and not for perfection. I am not a fan of these talent shows on television that seek out who is the best, and disillusion and condemn people who don't come up to the mark, according to the judges. This is continuing the damage of the music teachers I have mentioned previously, and stifling the natural spontaneity and creativity of our species.

Anyway, getting back to the training I was doing with the staff, the main thought that came out of the sessions was 'fun'. Having fun for the staff was such a change for them and essential to their being able to 'let go'. This had to remain my focus in preparing the combined session, for staff and residents to have fun, and to have fun together. Laughter brings healing and connects people. So I began my planning. I made up cassette tapes using a variety of musical styles, and keeping in mind what genre each of the staff had particularly enjoyed from the training. I made a compilation of classical music, waltzes, Scottish reels, big band sounds, cha chas, and folk dances with piano accordions and fiddles. I included military band marches, music from other cultures, flamenco, easy jazz, jives and pasa dobles. I wanted a combination of differing sounds and rhythms that would encourage movement.

The staff and I gathered together for the first ten minutes. We breathed, brought our focus into ourselves, how we were feeling, letting go of any worries and concerns, expanding our heart and our awareness to one another and thinking about our intention for the session. We had 15 minutes of songs on the piano, ably provided by our talented activities coordinator, and then I played songs on the guitar for a further 15 minutes. For the last 20 minutes I played the music I had recorded which finished with a gentle relaxed track, something like 'Albatross' (Fleetwood Mac 1969) or 'Cavatina' (Myers 1970).

Around the room I had laid out all the percussion instruments that I have, an abundance of coloured scarves of various shapes, sizes and textures, and an array of hats. I had also found some dance ribbons and cheerleader pom poms via the internet to try out. The purpose was for the staff and residents to connect with one another, singing and dancing in whatever way they wanted to, using percussion, scarves, hats, or not, as they chose. Most important, there was no right or wrong way of doing things, as long as we all moved and sang with love and held a loving intention to connect with one another. It was hilarious fun. The response from the residents was excellent and I was surprised many times by their reactions. The following are some highlights from my experiences.

Beattie does not always engage in my sessions; she is fully able but tends to wander, looking busy and intense. While I was playing my guitar near her, she stood up as if to leave the room. I took a chance and moved in front of her. She looked at the guitar, then my face, and to my surprise began to move a little, 'jigging' her upper body from side to side with the rhythm. I moved in the same way, still playing the guitar, mirroring Beattie's movements. As soon as I did, Beattie smiled a little and her movements grew larger. I followed her lead. Beattie exaggerated her dance even more. I did the same. She looked straight at me and I beamed, still singing. Beattie smiled wryly as though saying, 'See, I can join in when I fancy!' Then she began to mimic playing a guitar, both of us swinging away together. By the end of the song we looked like rock guitarists! I was thrilled to see Beattie so engaged, energized and enjoying our connection.

What was it that encouraged Beattie to join in instead of wandering? I think the one-to-one connection is important. We were dancing together, 'making a fool' of ourselves together. It is easier to dance with abandon with others doing the same, than on your own. Beattie was encouraged to join in because I was there for her. Through our dance Beattie expressed her playful nature. In these lively sessions, I don't feel as though I am being a fool. I love to feel free in the way I move, dance and sing, and being so abandoned encourages others, giving them permission, if you like, to do the same.

In the same session I danced with a lady called Rosa. I had only seen her once before, but not to talk with. I invited her to dance and she said she couldn't, probably because when we talk of dancing we generally imagine being on our feet, but no! Dancing can be as small as moving a little finger, or blinking an eye. It can be as large a gesture as leaping up and throwing our arms in the air. All movements can be considered a dance. As she wanted to remain seated, I suggested to Rosa that we dance with our arms, and demonstrated, offering my hands to her. Rosa took my hands in hers, and we swayed our arms from side to side with the music, holding hands gently. I was leading to start with, and then as I felt her movement grow stronger, I loosened one hand, and then the other. Rosa and I continued to dance separately but still facing one another. Now Rosa was leading and I reflected her movements; I followed her dance. With her arms raised above her head, Rosa bent deeply to one side then the other, and I copied. Rosa's movements were very graceful even to the ends of her fingers, and I felt sure she must have been a dancer. We kept strong eye contact through all this, both smiling and enjoying our connection. After the session I chatted with Rosa, and she talked about having a theatrical background. If we had not had this session I wonder where else she would have the opportunity to express her flowing grace and beauty in the movement of her body.

Staff need to express feelings

Dementia care can be exhausting. It requires many things from us to do it well. We need to be patient and intuitive as well as practical. Our role is to maintain contact with the inner person, all the while surmounting the often serious and difficult barriers to communication created by the damaged brain. We are frequently faced with considerable distress, extremely volatile emotions, illness and death. We need to find strong resources inside ourselves in order to meet the challenges of such work.

Defensively we may survive by keeping our distance. It is interesting that professionalism itself is often described as maintaining appropriate distance; we may say that the defence becomes institutionalized. But in dementia care such definition of professionalism needs to be challenged and changed. Where an essential professional goal is to strive to continue to see and listen to the person inside the condition, we need to be able to soften and make contact heart to heart within our professional role.

We may be hit by random emotional outbursts, we may be knocked by death. These shocks to the emotional system often make us close down, curl up, hide away with our emotions. We are protecting ourselves. Yet the work calls us to seek contact with the person inside the angry emotions, with the person who seems to be fading away. If we are to make contact, we have to be present, feeling and knowing our own emotions and able to reach out with them to others.

We imagine that if we become sensitive to our own emotions and those of others we may lose our dignity. 'I'm sorry that I'm crying. Let me pull myself together' are words that I sometimes hear. It is ironic that we should apologize for ourselves when we are deeply in touch with something important in our lives. Might it not be possible to re-perceive emotional vulnerability as strength, bringing us closer to the heart of humanity?

Clearly as professionals we need to be able to use emotions to good effect, for the benefit of the people in our care. Emotions bring us closer to the people we care for and they can inspire us to celebrate who a person was and is. There is a scared attitude to emotion in many of our so-called developed societies, a fear that emotions can be uncontrollable, destructive and chaotic. Yet emotions are the passionate proof of our investment in life, of our attachment to meaning and purpose. If we let ourselves feel them we can become invigorated in the work we do. We are brought closer to the value of our lives.

Supervision

Allowing ourselves to experience emotion, managing it and channelling it into our work must surely be a developmental goal for dementia care. Strong supervision needs to be in place as a container for such expansion of practice. Staff need to have a safe environment in which to express the issues and concerns arising from day-to-day experience in their setting. It is a way of letting go and moving on with increased insight and refined purpose.

Responding to death (some reflections by Sarah Povey)

Let's think about death for a little while. Not a subject that most of us want to dwell on, or in fact mention at all. It is one of those unspeakable subjects. Death is a word that, if you dare to say it, you say 'under your breath', in a whisper, looking embarrassed and apologetic. To speak about death seems to be taboo in our society and yet, as the saying goes, it is one of two things that you can be sure of in life. Let's face it, if you are working with older people, the chances are that when they leave you, it will be because they have died. It took me a while to properly consider this as, when I began my work with older people, I used to say as I left, 'Cheerio, see you next week' just as I might to my friends. Then I realized what a flippant comment this was, spoken without thought and consideration, not just to the individual but even more so to me. I needed to be aware that, when I said goodbye to someone I was singing with, it might indeed be the last time I spoke to them. I wanted to find a way to acknowledge that, just in case next time I went to see them they had died. I didn't want someone to die leaving me hanging, as it were, having spoken the promise of seeing them next week, next month or whenever it was. I needed to acknowledge the reality of our situation and our relationship. Each time I left I wanted to feel complete, settled in myself that nothing was left undone, there were no loose ends. It was important I ended each session with an easy feeling between the person with dementia and myself.

So, when I leave people now I say 'Goodbye' with the thought in mind that I may not see them again. This is simple. I don't make a 'song and dance' about it, nor will my statement of farewell seem 'over the top' to the individual either. It is me that holds the awareness. Of course, sometimes I am fortunate enough to know that someone is in the last few days or hours of their life and then I have the wonderful opportunity to say goodbye in song, as well as intention. For those of you who are experienced in care, you will be able to tell when someone is nearing the end of their life. I am fortunate to know some matrons and managers who will tell me when this is the case, so that I ensure I spend time with that individual on my visit. You may think that I should be able to recognize this myself, but with some people with dementia, they may be bedridden for some time. They may appear seemingly inanimate, but continue to live for years in this way, eating well, drinking well and appearing to do nothing else. Yes, I do find it difficult to see the approach of death and I appreciate the sharing of nursing experience that draws my attention to the arrival of someone's last moments. Sometimes I have thought that someone is dying and believed that on my next visit they will be gone, then I arrive the next week or month and they are still there. My error doesn't matter though if I am saying goodbye each time I leave.

Let me tell you about some of the occasions when I have been able to say a clear goodbye. I'll tell you about Mabel. I had known Mabel for only a few months and yet, from the first time I met her, she joined in singing with many of the songs. Sometimes the words came to her and sometimes not, but she always sang and smiled, as she joined in with the songs she recognized. Then, quite suddenly, her health deteriorated, she was restricted to her bed, being too weak to even sit up. I sang with her in her room a couple of times and then, on my next visit I learnt that she was dying. Her family was visiting and had asked if I would go and sing with them all. I was so humbled that the family would include me at such a special time. I came to Mabel's room and her daughter, Jane, was talking softly to her Mum, gently stroking her head. I was welcomed in, and once I had said hello to everyone, we talked about what to sing. We chose a song that we all knew and we sang together, a gentle, tender rendition of 'The Skye Boat Song' (Boulton 1884). Jane continued to softly stroke Mabel's head as we sang the song, like a lullaby. What a beautiful experience. Jane said afterwards that this gave her a treasured memory of her mother's last few hours and I was so pleased to have been able to do that. It is said that our hearing is the last of our senses to be lost when we die. For someone who enjoys music, I can think of no better way to make that journey, than be accompanied by singing, as you move from life to death and whatever lies beyond.

I imagine you thinking that you could never do that; could never sing with someone who is dying. Do you think you would feel silly, or do you worry about what other people might say or how they might judge you? Perhaps even being with someone who is dying is too overwhelming to contemplate. Well, it certainly isn't easy; the sense of grief can be strong. Even when I don't know someone well, even when they are not a part of my family, the emotional impact of being with someone who is dying is difficult. But oh, the beauty of the experience, if you just take a chance, is exquisite.

Grief especially makes singing difficult because as we sing we breathe life into our grief. Many of us are used to holding in our grief, and so if we are grieving and try to sing we find our voice getting caught in our throat, or feel that we dare not even take a breath for fear the grief, our tears, will rush out uncontrollably. I had an experience like this when my husband's grandmother, Edna, died. I had grown very close to her over the years, my own grandmother having died when I was 11. To have such a figure in my life when in my thirties was a great treasure for me. I stood at the front of the church at her funeral, and found myself overwhelmed by my feelings of grief and loss. As I tried to sing the first hymn 'Morning has Broken' (Farjeon 1931), my voice faltered, my throat tightened, and I tried to control myself. I became frustrated and angry. I did not want to deprive myself of this experience, this chance to honour the memory of times I had shared with 'Nan'. I wanted to say farewell to her, and yet, as I struggled to hold my emotions inside, I became less present to what was happening around me. Stifling my feelings was causing me physical pain so I vowed quietly to myself that I would sing out my feelings for Nan no matter how I sounded, or how others might perceive and judge me. I took a deep breath, and launched myself wholeheartedly into the hymn. I sang out as loud as I could, and though my voice faltered a few times, I continued on determinedly. Gradually I found more strength in my voice as my caught emotions found expression through the song. As I sang, the sense of being overwhelmed subsided, and I began to feel the love I held for Nan. I was singing of my love, my joy; using my voice to sound out my treasured memories of our times together, honouring her earthly life, her death, and singing her on to her next life. It was a moment of healing for me.

If you are with someone who is dying, and truly find it too daunting to sing yourself, then put on a CD, and hum along gently when you can. Your tears will undoubtedly flow, and don't be afraid of allowing that. You are losing someone you love, whether they are a relative or resident, and you have touched one another's lives for a short or long time. How long you have known one another is not important. It is the depth of feeling, the heartfelt connection you have made that is vital. 'Two may talk together under the same roof for many years, yet never really meet, and two others at first speech are old firends.' (Catherwood 1899, pp.6–7)

For those of us working with, or caring for older people, it is known that at some point we are going to have to say goodbye, that they are going to die. How sad that we are so squeamish about dealing with this openly. If you work in a care home I wonder how you deal with death. Do you have a plan at all? I don't mean the practical side, that is most likely to be clearly written down in a policy, and must be adhered to. Rather, I am thinking about the psychological side, both for the staff and for the residents. Everyone will have been emotionally engaged with an individual to some degree, naturally, as in our own social group, some more deeply than others. How do you let others in the home know that 'Vera' has died, that they won't be seeing her anymore? Do you say anything at all? Perhaps you don't say anything, and just let her vacancy be noticed. It is a quandary, and more so given our general reluctance to deal with death openly. Yet, whether anything formal is said or not, the loss of an individual will be felt and noticed by everyone.

I believe that every individual deserves to have their life, and their death, in this world acknowledged, and a chance should be given to all to say goodbye. It needn't be in a large gesture. One home I go to places a picture of the person who has died in the foyer, giving their name, and the years they were born and died. The first time I saw this, the picture was of a lady sitting happily in a garden chair toasting the photographer with a glass of wine. I did not know this lady, I had never met her, and yet I stopped for a moment, enchanted by her delightful photograph, and sent her a blessing. For a few seconds I was touched by her, we met across the barrier of the physical world, and then I continued on with my day. Letting people know who has died feels respectful. Even if that particular person was only known to visitors as 'the little chap that sits in the corner', it seems right to take a few moments to say farewell.

I was at one home recently when I found out a gentleman had died. I acknowledged this with the group I was singing with, and suggested that we sing his favourite song together. We did so, thinking of him, and then carried on. It was a loving moment, a fond moment, no big gestures, just enough to send our loving thoughts to him, and for a moment acknowledge too that we are all mortal, and our time will come.

I rather like the idea of a group of friends getting together to sing my favourite song after I am gone. I like the idea of being remembered, that people cared so much for me to do that even for a few moments.

Dementia care staff are dealing with death, most likely on a regular basis. What happens to your grief? How are your feelings dealt with and shared? Are they acknowledged or considered at all? What could be done to help you express how you are feeling? Getting the chance to say goodbye I believe is very important. If staff can say their farewells, before going off shift, to someone they know is deteriorating, I believe this will help. You could sit together and share your memories of that person: 'Do you remember that Jean would never eat peas without squishing them?' 'Peter always used to say "Good evening!" no matter the time of day.' 'Do you remember how Connie would shout until we got her singing "'My Old Man"?' (Leigh and Collins, early 20th century). Sharing memories in this way can be very healing; it breaks the silent taboo of death, and keeps the person alive in our hearts and minds. Everyone we care for, and work with, touches us in many ways. Even if we just found ourselves always annoyed with someone, still a connection has been made.

Evaluation of the dementia care project

The reflections on staff emotion in the presence of death and dying offered by Sarah above bring us back to the dementia care project (2008-2009) outlined at the beginning of the chapter with its emphasis on staff development. In evaluating the project let us remind ourselves of the research question: how can therapeutic relationships and environments that safeguard and enhance the wellbeing of older people with dementia be developed in social care services? Here, as we evaluate the creative arts component of the dementia care project, we ask the specific question: how can the creative arts contribute to therapeutic relationships and environments that safeguard and enhance the wellbeing of older people with dementia?

This question was answered clearly by participants who said that immersion in the stories of their partners through movement, dance, pictures and songs allowed them to escape from judgement, labelling and separation, so that they could really enjoy the cohabitation of experience, feeling and imagination together. From this place of non-division they were able to celebrate the human spirit in themselves and in others. The arts were said to give permission for feelings to be felt.

Because of this the arts seemed to the participants to breathe compassion into relationships and so helped participants to experience their partners as people rather then a set of categories.

Participants felt that their personal experience of a creative arts process cascaded down into their work with clients. Having felt the benefit of having their own internal experience validated by another person, staff felt more motivated to replicate this experience for their clients. Because they were more convinced of its value on a personal level, they showed a stronger commitment to pass it on to others.

Due to this positive personal experience of being witnessed and witnessing through the arts, staff felt confident in their enhanced ability to be open to the experience of others. They believed now in the value of meeting the other from a place of not knowing and not fixing. They felt strongly that it was only from this place of innocence that they would be able to see the other more clearly. By witnessing the movements, the singing, the dancing and the creative choices of the other from a place of not knowing, staff believed that they would be able to perceive the essence of others without limiting, confining and inaccurately pigeon-holing them.

To support their new-found confidence in instinctive emotional congruence and empathy, staff asked for creative supervision. The arts have the ability to contain and give expression to feelings, and there are many feelings present in dementia care. Sadness, pain and anger can easily arise when working with people with dementia. Learning how to both feel and contain emotions is a particular art which dementia staff need to develop if they are to learn how to be present and focused on the wellbeing of the person with dementia. By letting feelings out in supervision, we create the possibility of balance between presence and empathy in the workplace, as there is no need for personal catharsis at work if it has taken place in a safe supervisory context. Where there is a balance between professional support and professional duty, we build a strong staff team able to withstand the difficulties of the job and carry out responsibilities with conviction and confidence.

Finally by making space for compassion for both self and other, we build our practice on non-separation. With such a foundation the work becomes less about treating those less fortunate than ourselves and more about us all as humans. It becomes less patronizing and more humane. Ultimately it is less diminishing and more empowering for the recipient.

8

Conclusion

Listen, make contact and play

Yesterday I had a wonderful day; a day full of wonder. I spent the afternoon at one of the homes where Sarah works and took part in a 'Lively session'. Sarah took me in to the sun-filled lounge, a big room with orange carpets and orange curtains, comfortable chairs encircling the space and a piano in the centre. Lots of windows, lots of light.

Sarah moved around the room, sitting for a while with each person, introducing me to them. I noticed skin, translucent; I noticed blue, blue veins. I noticed bones. I noticed sore, red and swollen flesh. I noticed bodies curled over, shrunken from the world. I noticed automatic mannerisms. I noticed people sleeping, napping or switched off. Then I saw their eyes; eyes which were blank and misty, suddenly shine and focus, connecting with Sarah's gaze as she sat full and strong in front of them, holding their hands, saying 'Hello. It's Sarah who sings!' It was as if the soul had wandered away and was called back by the loving gaze, the desire for contact.

Sarah's eyes are very striking, big and bright, and unafraid. Sarah opens her eyes to others; she invites them with her eyes and her voice to join in the dancing and the singing. Some are reluctant, some don't seem to know her at first, but after a while they suddenly do know exactly who she is, they sigh and they say 'Ah yes…' and there is a softening in tone of voice and facial expression, an opening of the body.

Nancy is blind and hard of hearing. Sarah moves in close to her. Sarah's head and neck seem to dip down and find closeness to Nancy's face. Their heads are not touching, but their hair is brushed together. It is as if they are one. Nancy is speaking softly, Sarah's voice is gentle and soft. Sarah is talking to Nancy, telling her name, talking about singing and dancing. Nancy is nodding and smiling.

Mearns and Cooper (2006, p.40) give the analogy of the tuning fork for the process of relational depth in counselling and psychotherapy, 'the therapist's body and feelings resonating with the client's own physicality'. I believe that the writing on relational depth in therapy is applicable to person-centred practice, whether in therapy or care. Here, I was witnessing Sarah in this creative arts context as a tuning fork, making contact with another, listening with her eyes, ears and heart, giving the person her undivided attention and attuning herself to their shape and to their energy with her voice, her body, herself.

Rogers (1957) first gave us the concept of six core conditions in therapy, which facilitated client wellbeing, change and growth. These conditions are relevant to our dementia care context:

1. Two persons are in psychological contact.
2. The first, whom we shall call the client, is in a state of incongruence, being vulnerable or anxious.
3. The second person, whom we shall term the therapist, is congruent or integrated in the relationship.
4. The therapist experiences unconditional positive regard for the client.
5. The therapist experiences an empathic understanding of the client's internal frame of reference and endeavours to communicate this experience to the client.
6. The communication to the client of the therapist's empathic understanding and unconditional positive regard is to a minimal degree achieved. (Rogers 1957, p.96).

This must be our starting point in person-centred approaches to the creative arts. We are seeking to be in psychological contact with the person with dementia and we do this by listening in the ways described in this book following the wisdom imprinted in the Chinese character to listen (see page 6). To open up discussion on the process of listening, I have dwelt on the concept of 'witnessing' (see Introduction and Chapter 1), a concept which has been elaborated in the discipline of authentic movement (see Introduction) to include self-witnessing, becoming aware of thoughts, emotions and sensations which may get in the way of close empathic contact with the other. Such self-awareness is imperative for the development of unconditional positive regard, congruence and empathy, the three well-quoted elements of person-centred relationship.

Mearns and Cooper (2006, p.39) argue that 'A meeting at relational depth requires the therapist to be the unique, genuine human being that they are: a solid and grounded 'Otherness' with which the client can interact.' Such 'groundedness' can be developed through the creative arts, particularly the arts of movement and embodied practice (Chapter 2). By focusing into the body (Gendlin 1981) we come to feel fully our sensations, impulses and emotions and we can express them with mindfulness, taking responsibility for them. We come to appreciate our uniqueness, our difference. Then we can offer this in relationship with another. This is what I saw Sarah do yesterday in the 'Lively session'. She was offering herself, embodied, vital, passionate, alive. She received a response to this, constantly, as she moved around the room; her aliveness lit up the embers of aliveness in the other.

Sarah's congruence flowed into empathy at times as she noticed a response and blended with it. Yet all the time there was flux and flow, dynamic change: sometimes there was the strong presence of two different people responding joyfully and playfully to difference, for example, a little sparring game between partners with the great big colourful pompoms; and sometimes I witnessed blended, flowing movements in pairs, involved in the same rhythm.

The 'Lively session' began with the activities coordinator playing the piano. A series of old tunes were played, Strauss walzes, music hall songs. Immediately there was a transformation in the room. The television was switched off, there was a short silence and then the music. It seemed to me that people were set free. I was sitting next to Hilda, holding her hand. From being absent in her distanced, glazed face, she suddenly returned. Her eyes lit up. She immediately began to hum. I looked around and saw that the same thing had happened to several others. Their mouths were humming or singing the words. Their eyes were intent again. They were back!

Hilda began to move her hands. I caught the rhythm in my own. The music was enlivening us; bringing us to life. We gazed into each other's eyes and I felt like I was going to a deep place with Hilda, a place of the heart. We did not need any words. We were free, just enjoying the rhythm, enjoying the tune. It was lovely.

Now Sarah began to sing songs accompanied by her guitar. She has a beautiful strong voice, which carried round the room, inviting us all to join in. She sang many traditional songs, from Ireland, from Scotland, songs from Rodgers and Hammerstein films, songs from the music hall.

By now Hilda was recalling words and singing them to me. Lots of people were joining in, some adding little 'tra-las' as accompaniments between the lines. Sarah swept around the room, engaging people with her eyes, her voice, her movements. Members of staff were joining in too, enjoying the songs, doing the cancan, chuckling and laughing as their eyes met the eyes of their residents.

I felt like a child sitting there on the floor holding hands and singing with Hilda, crumbs of cake all around me on the carpet. It seemed to me that there was something very important in this feeling. For as a child it was easy to get lost in song, to be immersed in the moment of sound and movement. In this moment we are free from our attachments, from our worries, from our troubles, from times past and from times future. We could say that we are present with love, our essential nature.

After the singing came the dancing. Sarah put on some recorded music which she had compiled herself to include both the exotic and the familiar. We began with some Cuban-sounding dance music which caused me to jump up, move towards Linda and ask her to dance. She quietly asked me to pull her up and we began moving together, simply side to side holding hands. It was a very joyful feeling. We were together in the rhythm, our bodies responding to the music, alive, spontaneous. We were smiling, our eyes opening wider, taking in the room and the people in it.

The transformation in the room was evident. From a space of isolated inward-turning bodies, the room was now full of people who were gazing outwards and whose eyes were making contact with others, present and engaged. As we began to pack away the coloured scarves and musical instruments several people asked me 'Are you coming again next week? 'No? What a shame!' I could feel people really looking at me, taking me in, connecting with me. It felt great to move around the room, holding hands again with each person, looking into their eyes to say 'Goodbye.' I felt I had been on a journey into the heart and that this had been important. There was now a very different atmosphere. I felt people to be more settled and more present, calmer and happier. It had been a good session indeed.

A change of heart

To let ourselves experience our bodies, our hearts and our imaginations requires a sea change in our busy lives. To let ourselves slow down and 'be' with people, just sitting, holding hands, or singing and dancing, or making, we need to cultivate a different approach to care. Care in many contexts is about doing and fixing. Care of the soul, however, requires something else. It requires us to take time to drop our identities and meet people deeply in the place of the heart. This is a place of healing, a place of comfort.

Care such as this requires more resources. Quality of care is inextricably linked to the resourcing of care. Where there are more care staff, the pace of the day can slow down and we can make time to listen, connect and play. Yet while advocating for more resources, we can still seek to transform our situation within existing constraints. By committing ourselves to a person-centred approach, we make space for change to happen. If we believe in the value of person-centred dementia care and in the value of the creative arts as an essential part of such an approach, then we can invest in these things. I have been to many homes over the past few years where I have been amazed by the passion and commitment to person-centred care and to the creative arts. It is true that the creative arts already have a strong presence in many of our homes, but we can do more.

Remembering creativity

Let's remember what this book has been about. We began with creativity, an essential energy. Remember I wrote about the *repression* of creativity, which happens all too often in our Western cultures addicted to perfection. Oppressed by a particular model of artistic creativity, we lose confidence in our own inherent value and ability to dynamically express our lives through the arts. It has happened to us all to a greater or lesser extent on our march through life. We have all experienced that self-consciousness which brings the critical and controlling voice to bear upon our innate creativity: 'I can't draw, I can't sing, I can't dance.' And so we lose our spontaneity, our freedom, and we disconnect from our innate need to express our feelings through the arts.

The therapeutic use of the creative arts can help us to reconnect with this innate need because in a therapeutic context there is no requirement to comply with fixed models of aesthetic beauty. We are simply having fun expressing ourselves. We are enjoying the sound, the movement, the colour, as an internally-felt experience. We do not need to conform. We are in true relationship with the arts medium and nothing else matters.

It is exciting to see people coming to life again through such joyful experience of the arts. For whenever we really listen to a song, or let ourselves deeply experience colour and shape, or begin to move and dance with internal awareness, the old creativity is right there waiting. We are drawn back into the tide.

It is vital that as carers we are in touch with our own creativity if we are to bring creative approaches and ideas to people with dementia. It is no use going through the motions of an arts activity if we are not feeling the internal ripples of the song, the dance, the picture. If we can let ourselves be really present with our hearts and bodies and immerse ourselves in the arts activities, we will meet others there in the place of the heart.

Remembering embodiment

In Chapter 2, I looked at meditation and the body in dementia care. Cultivating a meditative attitude (Silverton 2009) to care is aligned with care of the soul. A meditative attitude is interested in the *quality* of experience rather than the measurement of experience. A meditative approach is concerned with felt-sense, congruence and empathy whereas a calculative approach (Silverton 2009) depends upon objective observation and aims to match behaviour with established patterns.

A meditative approach can be promoted through embodiment. If we take time at the beginning of the day to stretch out, to do a few yoga exercises or t'ai chi sequences, we bring ourselves home to our bodies. We begin to cultivate an internal awareness of our bodies and to feed them; we begin to appreciate and look after ourselves. Wouldn't it be wonderful if we could start the day as a staff group with a short 'movement and stillness' session? We would awaken our awareness of our bodies and minds through gentle movement, quietly observing sensations and thoughts with a peaceful accepting attitude. Movement can lead to stillness in this way, helping us to be present and anchored, ready for depth connection.

The expressive body tells us a lot about ourselves and about others. It expresses how we are feeling inside. Our posture, our full body movement or lack of it, our gestures, all show dynamically and energetically how we feel and think. Often our bodies get caught in traps of ritualized, automatic movement. We end up moving in established patterns with little freedom for expression. This is true for us all, but all the more true for people whose bodies are overtaken by diseases where reflex movements control them. By bringing expressive movement and dance into the daily programme in your dementia care setting, you can begin to loosen the grip of automatic movement and to encourage creativity in the body. Carried by the music, the person can experience their expressive potential through their body's innate responsiveness to sound and to song.

Remembering person-centred approaches and ideas in the creative arts

Our fundamental premise has been that person-centred practice requires us to appreciate the *person* with dementia. It is this personhood that we are trying to meet and to support through our use of the arts in dementia care. We believe that despite the damage done to the brain by dementia, the heart, the core, the essence of the person is still there. As my friend, whose mother had dementia, says, 'Intuition remains when the mechanics have gone.' When we play music or dance, or show an image, painting or a photograph to people without language or memory, they are able to respond from a deep intuitive place, which I have been calling 'heart'. This is why the arts can help to maintain and nurture our personhood in dementia; no language is needed to experience, feel and express our heart. We can express heart through a gesture, a look, a sound, a colour.

We all have affinities with different arts media. Sarah's is voice and movement: she is at home with singing and dancing; mine is the expressive body, imagery and story: I am at home with moving, dancing and story-making. You will also know which arts you like best, and if you are facilitating a creative arts session, it is wise to begin with an art which you love. Your love of the art will influence the energy and outcome of the session. Your love of the art will enhance the meeting which takes place in the creative process.

Remembering existential approaches to the creative arts

I have been emphasizing the importance of acceptance in dementia care. I feel that it is vital in all therapeutic work to really listen to the person without any agenda for change. I believe that when a person feels truly listened to and accepted they will find what they need to live healthfully. This approach does not change when we meet the person with dementia. Feelings need a safe haven, a receptacle, so that they can be laid down and released. By acknowledging someone's feelings we help them to find a safe haven.

Sarah gave examples in Chapter 3 of people with dementia laying feelings to rest. Often there is a sense of things being replayed over and over again from the past. We can help a person to let go of these old feelings and situations by listening and also by depicting them in the arts, perhaps in a song, perhaps in a movement, perhaps in a picture. It is vital that we accept the feelings just as they are. Even if we think that the stories have been made up, we still need to accept the feelings expressed because they are what matters. The person is communicating something about their present emotional state, which may or may not be attached to a past event.

We do not try to steer the creative process in a particular way. It is important that we witness the person as they participate, that we facilitate *their* expression. We need to stay 'present' (see Chapter 2) and involved, ready to interact, but this does not mean we dominate and control the process. We interact congruently and sensitively with the other seeking to encourage *their* creativity.

The stigma of dementia

I have noticed that when 'disease' strikes I am suddenly 'on the edge'. Because there is something 'wrong' with me, because I am 'different', I no longer live in the mainstream, I am drifting to the edge. My bond with others is undone because I represent something they would not wish to happen to themselves.

Until we climb inside the lives of others and accept that their story is ours too, we cannot hope to overcome the stigma of illness and disease. Disease is part of human life, just as it is part of nature. There is no stigma to disease but the one we give it from our own prejudice (Ramsay *et al.* 2002).

By separating ourselves from people with dementia we take away our opportunity to meet them where they are. We need to reframe our perception of dementia if we are to join with them. Dementia is not something which happens to others and not us, or other people's families and not ours. Dementia can hit any one of us at any time; it is part of the human condition. Only when we include dementia in a holistic conceptualization of life can we begin to work with it as part of life. For dementia is a condition of the *living*: people with dementia are *living with* dementia, not *dying from* it. When we begin to perceive dementia in *this* way, we can embrace life with dementia wholeheartedly; our motivation to improve the quality of life for people with dementia becomes stronger.

Quality of life and the creative arts

The creative arts improve our quality of life in many ways. They can make us feel better. They improve our mood, they soothe us, they enliven us, they bring back memory and desire, they enlighten us, they help things to fall into place. It is no different for people with dementia. When words are failing or vanishing the arts can still restore us. They reach us in a place beyond words. Music still touches us deeply. As one woman in the early stages of dementia said, 'I don't know what happened but the music got inside my body and I just had to dance.'

We can still feel textures, we can still feel a rhythm, we can still feel emotionally affected by colours and aromas when words are difficult to speak and understand. The creative arts provide a realm for the senses. The senses are soothed or enlivened through the creative arts. The creative arts meet the sensory body's need for wellbeing.

The creative arts also touch our inner lives, our invisible emotions. Sensation arouses emotion and memory so we can make contact with our hearts and times past through the arts. Unresolved moments can be expressed through the arts and laid to rest, or warm and loving moments can caress us again and make us feel good.

The arts endure. They provide a thread to our deeper lives. They join us together. They create community. Singing and dancing together creates a sense of unity and solidarity in suffering and joy.

Our relationship with people with dementia

The sense of unity inspired by the creative arts can have a powerful effect upon relationship between people with dementia and their families and their staff. When we join together through song and dance, we perceive each other differently, we touch each others' hearts (see page 6), and this deepens our contact with each other. We are changed by this deep relationship. We find stillness (Boxhall 1999). It is as if by feeling the song and dance we are put in touch with something which is deeply moving, and it is our impulse to express it. In joint expression we link deeply with another and find this place of stillness together. This contact with the heart nurtures our own lives just as it nurtures the lives of people with dementia.

Joint practice and teamwork

We have found that joint practice, a term we use for empathic contact and meeting at depth levels of being, is beneficial to all people involved with dementia care. Staff who took part in our Skills for Care creative arts training noticed that they understood each other better as a result of the activities and felt that this would enhance their working together as a team. Understanding and teamwork are essential in dementia care where the work is both physically and emotionally very demanding.

In one home there was so much grief as people identified links between the people in the home and their own grandparents. There were a lot of tears and so much love. In expressing these feelings through movement and drawing, the staff were able to reach a clearer consciousness of how they were affected by their work. They listened with respect to each other's feelings as they described and explained the pictures they had made after the movement work. They gained a new understanding both of themselves and of each other. They felt they could support each other better as a result of this sharing.

In another home, staff were surprised how much was communicated about feelings through movement and gesture. They experienced how deep bodily communication could be, as they witnessed each other and then replayed in their own body movement what they had perceived. The partner invariably felt deeply listened to, yet no words had been spoken.

In yet another home there were many tensions arising from misunderstanding between cultures. The creative arts training gave people the opportunity to talk about their feelings of being away from home, of being in a strange culture, of feeling awkward and embarrassed by the expectation to behave differently. Through this expression of inner feelings people were able to understand and help each other better instead of criticizing from a place of ignorance.

Experiences such as these not only provided food for thought in re-perceiving people with dementia, but clearly enabled the staff to re-perceive one another. Using the arts of movement and drawing in this instance had helped people to stand back from their habitual way of being and to cultivate a more empathic and meditative attitude towards one another. When staff are working as a team, having had the opportunity to ease tensions arising from misunderstanding, the atmosphere in the home will be different. The atmosphere of acceptance will pervade throughout the home and the residents will benefit from it.

A review of the current situation in dementia care

Rebecca Wood, Chief Executive of the Alzheimer's Research Trust, observes that the dementia care system is 'antiquated' and 'lags far behind achievements in medicine and care elsewhere' (cited in Lord 2009). Dinah Lord (2009), Executive Producer of the Gerry Robinson (2009) broadcasts on dementia care writes, 'In the next 20 years over a million of us will have dementia. This is a frightening statistic. What I find equally staggering, however, is the reluctance to confront the state of dementia care in this country [UK].' Tony Robinson's documentary (2005) reflects upon the concept of a 'home' for people with dementia, and rejoices in the rare context of a home where the manager and her family live with the occupants and life is integrated, like in one large family. In this particular context, which is sheltered housing for elderly people who do not have dementia, activities take place every night and often outrageous fun is had by all. There is lots of laughter in an atmosphere of belonging together. Robinson (2005) acknowledges that this integrated living would be more difficult in dementia care but that it is something to aim for. Entrepreneur Gerry Robinson's (2009) investigation into dementia care *Can Gerry Robinson Fix Dementia Care Homes?*, suggests that integration rather than separation is a much more successful way of promoting the wellbeing of people with dementia. When staff wore their own clothes rather than a uniform and ate their meals with residents, a sense of family and home was created. Residents clearly benefited emotionally and psychologically from such an approach because they seemed happy and calm in this context.

The link to the creative arts

The ideas which spring from these programmes fit very well with the message of this book. I have been advocating empathy and integration in our work with creative arts. We need to make the link between ourselves and people with dementia if we are to put our weight into integrated practice. We need to acknowledge that we thrive much better when we feel we belong and when we feel we are loved. The creative arts are a good way of expressing love and belonging simply, through patient sharing of music, song, movement, dance, pictures, stories.

Lord (2009) quotes Robinson:

> We want to believe, perhaps need to believe, that our loved ones are in some kind of happy fuzzy state in homes where they are well cared for and looked after night and day. The stark reality is that, for most people, that cosy picture is a long way from the truth. (Robinson 2009)

We need to make our homes like real homes so that people with dementia feel that they are loved and that they belong, particularly as these qualities of love and belonging are the ones which hold us together in this stage of our lives.

We can easily communicate loving connection through the creative arts because when we are being creative together we are not trying to change, fix or control the other; rather, we are accepting our common bond and we are accepting each other as we are. This is the first step towards true integration. When we see ourselves as essentially the same deep down, there are no barriers and we understand that when we witness someone we are also witnessing ourselves.

In the creative arts we are putting our faith in something which is beyond human control. We are putting our faith in creativity as a healing process. It is true that when we let go of our rational mind and we allow spontaneous creative process to come alive, we are often surprised by our experience. We learn something which we could not have 'thought'. We perceive other things: things about our bodies and the bodies of others; things about our feelings, our emotions, and those of other people; things about our embodied and feeling connection with the other. We may be amazed by the intuitive life we sense in the person with dementia, we may be surprised by the beauty of the ageing body. When we give up our desire to make something other than what it is, when we accept the present without resistance or denial, we see things as they are, we are open to what the present is offering us.

Lord (2009) comments on the need for sensory stimulation in dementia care. She notices that people with dementia are much happier if they have something to feel, to play with. She recommends placing toys and dolls and everyday objects around the home, so people can pick them up and handle them easily. This observation was also made in

Tony Robinson's (2005) documentary where having objects and fabrics to touch and move was equated with contentment. In creative arts work we use sensory stimulation all the time, bringing in fabrics and objects to soothe and to stimulate body and mind. Trueman (2009) points to the widespread use of psychotic drugs in the control of mental state in dementia. He advocates mental stimulation as an alternative to the use of psychotic drugs, which can change someone overnight into a different person. The creative arts can provide mental stimulation through sensory channels, awakening thought, memory and emotion.

Lord (2009) regrets the lack of training for dementia care staff. She writes about 'a culture of stagnant lounges, a lack of specialist training among staff, and a focus on keeping people alive, rather than helping them to live a happy life.' These last two aspects of dementia care are certainly related. If staff receive specialist training, they will be able to connect with people with dementia more easily and the wellbeing of people with dementia will be increased.

The emphasis in dementia care needs to on be on 'living a full life' (Robinson 2005) and so training needs to concentrate on how to help people with dementia live full lives. This is where the creative arts have an important part to play. As we have seen, the creative arts have the capacity to create relationship and to bring people to life, to facilitate their experience of heartfelt connection and joy.

The healing capacity of the arts

The creative arts act as carriages for our feelings; people with dementia, families, friends and staff can all benefit from the creative arts in their capacity to carry and hold all sorts of feelings, painful and joyful. The arts through their symbolism and sensory nature help us to bear the feelings; they bring them into the body and the heart where they can be experienced fully and then breathed out. If we do not do this and feelings remain unprocessed in the realm of thought, we never feel them as part of us and they control us from a disembodied distant place. It is important that we share our feelings so that we no longer feel isolated and alone, and in emotional pain and conflict. Being together with our feelings can help to heal us.

'The silent community'

This book has been written for 'the silent community' (Robinson 2005), a community of people with dementia, their families, friends and staff, a community who needs much more support from our governments to create a culture of 'care based on love' (Robinson (2005). Sarah and I would say that we need to develop a culture of love and listening in dementia care and that this can be enhanced through our use of the creative arts. When we focus on love and listening in our use of the creative arts, we create the opportunity for people with dementia to live a stimulating and full life. We contribute towards their future as well as providing a dignified ending to their lives. In future years, care of the elderly must become a national priority and we hope that the creative arts will provide a significant contribution to the lives of older people in the many different forms described and illustrated in this book.

A thank you for 'being with'

As a final note I would like to share a recent experience in hospital when I was having major surgery. Immobilised and in pain I was fortunate enough to be washed by one of the ancillary staff, who treated me with respect and dignity. She made no reference to my condition, she simply treated me as a human being, a person. She gently washed my arms and hands, my upper chest and back, my face. There was no rush, there was simply *being*. She was simply *being with* me in the moment, accepting me as I was, and accepting our connection. It was a loving experience and one which soothed and healed me. I am grateful for this gift.

It may be that we consider this little story as insignificant, but it is not. For it was in this moment that I knew how important it is for the witness to be with the person in difficulty. We can deliver many actions to someone day to day, but then we are probably treating their bodies and not their souls, and this means that we abandon them again and again to their lonely internal world. We need to try to make links with the ones who seem agitated and in emotional pain. The creative arts and the meditative body are powerful ways of linking us together through shared stimulating or soothing sensory experience.

The author

Jill Hayes

Jill Hayes is a practitioner, teacher, writer and researcher in the field of the creative arts. Originally training in the 'life-art method' with Daria Halprin, Jill has adapted her person-centred approach to the creative arts therapies to make it more accessible to a variety of populations. Jill is passionate about the capacity of the creative arts to create empathy and understanding between people, and for this reason actively promotes its use in qualitative research as a way of knowing about the lives of others. She has written a book (see References) which shows how performing people's lives can lead to healing. It has been a real joy for Jill to write this book in close collaboration with her colleague Sarah Povey (Chapter 3 and contributions to Chapters 6 and 7), and in consultation with her colleague Carly Marchant, whose case study in Chapter 7 adds sparkles of light and love.

The contributors

Carly Marchant

In her role as a registered movement psychotherapist, Carly Marchant, acts as a practitioner in treating individuals, an entrepreneur in establishing her business in psychotherapy, and a researcher especially interested in autistic spectrum disorders. Carly believes strongly that every individual has a right to communication and inclusion, no matter how severe the barriers they face. The expressive arts permit communication through channels other than the primary, and sometimes impossible, medium of talking. Through the expressive arts Carly sees the possibility of overcoming communication barriers and social exclusion in such conditions as autistic spectrum disorders and Alzheimer's disease.

Sarah Povey

Sarah Povey has been singing all her life with church, school, college and community choirs. Even as a child she used to sing herself to sleep. Fascinated by the healing aspects of the voice, she was attracted to a course developed by Paul Newham and trained as a voice movement therapy practitioner with him, qualifying in 1999. Since then, Sarah has been further enhancing her skills and expertise working with older people, both with and without dementia, and with people with learning difficulties. She currently works in homes across West Sussex and Hampshire applying techniques she has shared in this book.

Literature references

Alzheimer's Society (2007) *Dementia UK: Summary of Key Finding.* London: Alzheimer's Society. Available at www.alzheimers.org.uk/site/scripts/download_info.php?fileID=1, accessed on 1 July 2010.

Barry, S. (2008) *The Secret Scripture.* London: Faber & Faber.

Blake, W. 'Auguries of Innocence', quoted in Malcolmson, A. (ed.) (1967) *William Blake: An Introduction.* London: Constable Young Books Ltd.

Boxhall, M. (1999) 'Working from Stillness'. *Stillness.* Available at www.stillness.co.uk/about_stillness.php, accessed 27 March 2010.

Bradford Dementia Group at Bradford University, www.bradford.ac.uk/acad/health/dementia

Buber, M. (1996) *I and Thou.* New York. NY: Touchstone.

Cameron, J. (1995) *The Artist's Way: A Course in Discovering and Recovering Your Creative Self.* London and Basingstoke: Pan Books.

Catherwood, M. (1899) 'Marianson.' In *Mackinac and Lake Stones.* New York: Harper & Brothers..

Chodorow, J. (ed.) (1997) *Jung on Active Imagination.* Princeton, NJ: Princeton University Press.

Cooper, M. (2001) 'Embodied Empathy.' In S. Haugh and T. Merry (eds) *Empathy.* Ross-on-Wye: PCCS Books.

Dissanayake, E. (1997) 'Movement, Time, and Emotional Communication.' *Proceedings 30th Annual Conference Congress on Research 30,* 1–2. Tucson, AZ: The Congress on Research in Dance.

Forrester, C. (2007) 'Your own body of wisdom: recognizing and working with somatic countertransference with dissociative and traumatized patients.' *Body, Movement and Dance in Psychotherapy 2,* 2, 123–33.

Frank, A.W. (1995) *The Wounded Storyteller: Body, Illness and Ethics.* Chicago, IL: University of Chicago Press.

French, C. Unpublished poem, 'Villanelle – with apologies to Dylan Thomas.'

Fry, S. (2005) *The Ode Less Travelled: Unlocking the Poet Within.* London: Hutchinson.

Gendlin, E. (1981) *Focusing.* New York: Bantam.

Gordon, R. (1975) 'The Creative Process: Self Expression and Self-Transcendence.' In S. Jennings (ed.) *Creative Therapy.* London: Pitman.

Goswami, A. (2009) 'God is not dead.' *Resurgence 256,* 20–22.

Halprin, A. (1995) *Moving Toward Life.* Hanover, NH: Wesleyan University Press.

Halprin, D. (2003) *The Expressive Body in Life, Art and Therapy.* London: Jessica Kingsley Publishers.

Hammond, R. (2007) *On the Edge: My Story.* London: Weidenfeld and Nicolson.

Hartley, L. (2004) *Somatic Psychology: Body, Mind and Meaning*. London and Philadelphia: Whurr Publishers.

Hayes, J. (2004) 'The Experience of Student Dancers in Higher Education in a Dance Movement Therapy Group, with Reference to Choreography and Performance.' Unpublished PhD, University of Hertfordshire.

Hayes, J. (2007) *Performing the Dreams of Your Body: Plays of Animation and Compassion*. Chichester: Archive Publishing.

Innes, A. and Hatfield, K. (eds) (2004) *Healing Arts Therapies and Person-Centered Dementia Care*. London: Jessica Kingsley Publishers.

Jung, C.G. (1990) *Memories, Dreams, Reflections*. London: Fontana Paperbacks.

Jung, C. G. (1979) 'The Spirit in Man, Art and Literature'. *The Collected Works of C.G. Jung*, Vol. 15. London: Routledge and Kegan Paul.

Kitwood, T. (1997) *Dementia Reconsidered: The Person Comes First*. Philadelphia, PA: Open University Press.

Lawrence, D.H. (1963) 'Shadows.' *Selected Poems*. Harmondsworth: Penguin.

Levine, S. (2009) *Trauma, Tragedy and Therapy: The Arts and Human Suffering*. London: Jessica Kingsley Publishers.

Lewis, P. (1993) *Creative Transformation: The Healing Power of the Arts*. Wilmette, IL: Chiron Publications.

Lord, D. (2009) 'Dementia care "failing" the elderly.' BBC News 8 December 2009. Available at http://news.bbc.co.uk/1/hi/health/8399760.stm, accessed on 27 March 2010.

Mahler, M.S. and Furer, M. (1968) *On Human Symbiosis and the Vicissitudes of Individuation*. New York: International Universities Press.

Malcolmson, A. (ed.) (1967) *William Blake: An Introduction*. London: Constable Young Books Ltd.

McNiff, S. (2004) *Art Heals: How Creativity Cures the Soul*. Boston, MA: Shambhala Productions.

Mearns, D. and Cooper, M. (2006) *Working at Relational Depth in Counselling and Psychotherapy*. London: Sage.

Moore, T. (1994) *Care of the Soul: A Guide for Cultivating Depth and Sacredness in Everyday Life*. New York: HarperPerennial.

Musicant, S. (1994) 'Authentic Movement and Dance Therapy.' *American Journal of Dance Therapy 16*, 2, 91–106.

Musicant, S. (2001) 'Authentic movement: Clinical considerations. *American Journal of Dance Therapy 23*, 1, 17–26.

Newham, P. (1999) *Using Voice and Movement in Therapy*. London: Jessica Kingsley Publishers.

O'Donohue, J (1999) *Anam Cara: Spiritual Wisdom From the Celtic World*. London: Bantam.

Payne, H. (ed.) (2006) *Dance Movement Therapy: Theory, Research and Practice*. London: Routledge.

Pearmain, J. (2001) *The Heart of Listening: Attentional Qualities in Psychotherapy*. London: Continuum.

Ramsay, R., Page, A., Goodman, T. and Hart, D. (eds) (2002) *Changing Minds: Our Lives and Mental Illness*. London: Gaskell.

Rogers, C.R. (1957) 'The necessary and sufficient conditions of therapeutic personality change.' *Journal of Consulting Psychology 21*, 2, 95–103.

Rogers, C.R. (1996) 'Experiences in Communication.' In *A Way of Being*. New York: Houghton Mifflin Company.

Royal College of Psychiatrists (2009) *Alzheimer's Disease and Dementia.* Available at www.rcpsych.ac.uk/default.aspx?page=1427, accessed on 25 March 2010.

Sidney, De hann Research Centre for Arts and Health http://www.canterbury.ac.uk/centres/sidney-de-haan-/research/index.asp

Silverton, S. (2009) 'Heartbreak Hotel.' *Self and Society 37,* 1, 20–30.

Stern, D. (1985) *The Interpersonal World of the Infant: A View from Psychoanalysis and Developmental Psychology.* New York: Basic Books.

Stern, D (2004) *The Present Moment in Psychotherapy and Everyday Life.* New York: W.W. Norton.

Thich Nhat Hanh (2009) 'Indra's net.' *Resurgence 256,* 18–19.

Trueman, A. (2009) 'He Became a Different Person.' BBC News 12 November 2009. Available at http://news.bbc.co.uk/1/hi/health/8355535.stm, accessed on 27 March 2010.

Whitehouse, M. (1999) 'Jung and Dance Therapy.' In P. Pallaro (ed.) *Authentic Movement: Essays by Mary Starks Whitehouse, Janet Adler and Joan Chodorow.* London: Jessica Kingsley Publishers.

Whitton, E. (2003) *Humanistic Approach to Psychotherapy.* Chichester: John Wiley and Sons.

Winnicott, D.W. (1985) *Playing and Reality.* London: Pelican.

Woodman, M. (1993) *Conscious Femininity.* Toronto: Inner City Books.

Music references

Baring-Gould, S. (lyrics) (1865) and Sullivan, A. (music) (1871) 'Onward Christian Soldiers.' In *Songs of Fellowship*. Eastbourne: Kingsway Music.

Berlin, I. (1942, first written 1940) 'White Christmas.' Decca Records.

Boulton, Sir H. (lyrics) (1884) traditional tune 'The Skye Boat Song.' London: Boulton and MacLeod.

Coborn, C. (1886) 'Two Lovely Black Eyes.' In *Francis & Days's Popular Song Books*. London: Francis, Day & Hunter.

Donaldson, W. (music) and Kahn, G. (lyrics) (1928) 'Makin' Whoopee!'

Farjeon, E. (lyrics 1931) 'Bunessan,' (Music) 'Morning has Broken.'

Fleetwood Mac (1969) 'Albatross.' Blue Horizon.

Hazlewood, L. (1966) 'These Boots Are Made for Walkin'.' *Boots*. Reprise Records.

Kander, J, (music) and Ebb, F. (lyrics) (1977) 'New York, New York.' *New York, New York*. Reprise Records.

Kellette J. (music) and Kenbrovin, J. (lyrics) (1919) 'I'm Forever Blowing Bubbles.' Kendis-Brockman Music Co.

Kennedy, J. (circa 1939–40) 'We're Going to Hang Out the Washing on the Siegfried Line.'

Krull, A., Roederer, M., Bauer, T., Lukhaup, C., Schmidt, M. and Espena Es Krull, L.K. (2004) 'For Amelie.' *Lovelorn*. Germany: Hanseatic Musikverlag.

Lauder, L. and Grafton, G. (1905) 'I Love a Lassie.' In *Francis & Day's Popular Song Book*. London: Francis, Day & Hunter.

Leigh F. W. and Collins, C. (early 20th century) 'My Old Man (Said Follow the Van).' *One More Time* (1985) In International Music Publications.

Lennon, J. and McCartney, P. (1963) 'I Want to Hold Your Hand.' Parlophone and Columbia Records.

Lennon, J. and McCartney, P. (1967) 'Penny Lane.' Parlophone and Columbia Records.

Lyte, H.F. (lyrics 1847) and Monk, W.H. (music 'Eventide' 1861) 'Abide with Me.'

MacColl, E. (1957) 'The First Time Ever I Saw Your Face.'

Moore, C. (1989) 'The First Time Ever I Saw Your Face.' *Voyage*. WEA Records Ltd.

Myers, S. (1970) 'Cavatina.' CD Classic FM 'Relax More'

Newton, J. (lyrics 1779) and Walker, W. (set words to tune 'New Britain' 1835) 'Amazing Grace.' In *Songs of Fellowship*. Eastbourne: Kingsway Music.

Powell, G.H. (lyrics) and Powell, F. (music) (1915) 'Pack Up Your Troubles in Your Old Kit-Bag, and Smile, Smile, Smile.'

Richard, C. and The Shadows (1963) 'Summer Holiday.' Columbia Records.

Rodgers, R. (music) and Hammerstein II, O. (lyrics) (1943) 'Oh What a Beautiful Mornin'.' *Oklahoma! Vocal Score* New York: Williamson Music.

Rodgers, R. (music) and Hammerstein II, O. (lyrics) (1959) 'Edelweiss.' *In* Lindsay, H. and Crouse, R. (1995) *The Sound of Music–Vocal Score.* New York.

Sinatra, N. (1966) 'These Boots Are Made for Walkin' *Boots.* Reprise Records. In MacMahon, D. (1957) *The New National and Folk Song Book.* London: Nelson.

Unknown author and date. 'Widdecombe Fair.'

Unknown author (tune circa 1728) 'English Country Garden.' In Lavender, P. (1995) *New Songs for Children.* London: Wise Publications.

Unknown author (circa 1841) 'Loch Lomond.' In MacMahon, D. (1957) *The New National and Folk Song Book.* London: Nelson.

Weatherley, F. (lyrics), tune 'Londonderry Air' (1913) 'Danny Boy.' In Turner, M.R. and Miall, A. (1982) *The Edwardian Song Book.* London: Methuen.

Weston, H. and Lee, B. (1938) 'Knees Up Mother Brown.' Sheet music available at www.musicnotes.com

Whiting, R.A. and Akst, H. (music) and Jahn, G. (lyrics) (1931) 'Guilty.' *Die Farbelhafte Welt der Amelie* (2001) France: Virgin Records.

Williams, H. (music) and Kennedy, J. (lyrics) (1935) 'Red Sails in the Sunset.' Decca Records.

Yorkston, J. (1884) 'Cockles And Mussels.' London: Francis Brothers and Day.

Television and film references

Jeunet, J.P. (dir) (2001) *Amélie.* UGC Images, Tapioca Films, France 3 Cinema, MMC Independent.

Perry, J. and Croft, D. (1968–77) *Dad's Army.* London: BBC.

Robinson, G. (2009) *Can Gerry Robinson Fix Dementia Care Homes?* BBC2, 8 December 2009. Available at www.bbc.co.uk/programmes/b00pccch, accessed on 27 March 2010.

Robinson, T. (2005) *Me and My Mum.* Channel 4. Available at www.channel4.com/programmes/tony-robinson-me-and-my-mum, accessed on 27 March 2010.

Subject Index

Author Index